I can still hear what

Grandma Said

"Give me my flowers while I live"

Sonya JW Lunsford

I can still hear what Grandma Said
"Give me my flowers while I live"
Copyright © 2015 by Sonya JW Lunsford

ISBN 978-0-692-66750-7

Dedication

I wrote this book in Memory
Of
Our Grandmother, Mother Selema P. Berry who
made her Television Debut in the For Us the Living: The
Medgar Evers Story 1983 · Drama/Biography as an
extra in the Church scene

This book is dedicated
To
My very Supportive Husband,
John P. Lunsford Sr.,
Our children
Samantha E. Lunsford and John P. Lunsford Jr.,
And my Parents
Sandra J. Warner and Major L. Warner Sr.
To my Nephews and Nieces, I hope this book
encourages you to set your goals and reach them with
the help of your faith in God

Acknowledgement

The most giving, caring, intelligent, wise, kind hearted, beautiful, dedicated, determined, God fearing, loving woman I know, my Mother Sandra J. Warner, without you this book would not be. From my heart to yours, Thank You and I Pray God continue to bless you with great strength, wisdom, health, wealth, and love with His Hand of mercy and grace, as He has always and more!

My Father, Mr. Major L. Warner Sr. who has always encouraged me to be whom I was born to be. Your words of wisdom are always needed and wanted. I could always feel your presence and hear your voice. Your one and only daughter, I love you Dad!

The God sent man of God, my Husband, John P. Lunsford, Sr. There is no other who could fit me the way you do. I thank God each day for you. Your unwavering love through support has kept me strong in my faith. Man I love you!

The God sent "Life Changers"; our daughter Samantha E. Lunsford and our son John P. Lunsford Jr. God used each of you to save me. I am here to write this book because of you. The feedback you gave helped point me in the right direction. God really used you both. Thanks! Mother loves you!

My Big Momma, Mrs. Sallie E. Warner, thanks for the prayers and your influence on me while writing this book and more. I Thank God you are in my life, a part of my life, and because of you I have life. I love and adore you. My dear Grandmother, thanks for sharing your life with me. The way you shared yourself has allowed me to see myself.

My four (4) brothers, Mr. Major, L. Warner Jr.,
Mr. Morton T. Warner Sr., and
Sergeant Robert N. Warner Sr., I love and thank you. Specially Thanks to my little brother Mr. Claude Weaver III for your input on this book.

To my Aunts, Uncles, Cousins, God sent Sisters, Brothers and Friends, who pray for me that I would walk in the purpose God has for me, Thanks! Please continue to lift me up to God, for it is only God who orders my steps.

Table of Contents

9) I'm Just Saying

Introduction

Do you find yourself trying to remember what your Grandma said? Perhaps you are like me. I can remember some of the words but not all of them. I came to realized that my memory of what Grandma said came easier when I applied what Grandma said. I would find myself during discussions with others saying, my Grandmas said this, and my Grandma said that; more often than not. I realized there are many who had not heard of what Grandma said. They were hearing it for the first time. Even family members. There are also those who will never admit they have forgotten or never knew what Grandma said. Then there are those who have heard, but have trouble remembering complete statements of what Grandma said. It suddenly came clear to me. I should write it all down.

For years I did not write but I continued saying Grandma said this, Grandma said that, during my daily life! One day during prayer a small still voice came to me. "Sonya write". I thought, write what. "Write it all down". "It" being the words of wisdom God has allowed to guide me to this point. So that is what I began doing, writing. Grandma said is filled with words to live by, which will hopefully inspire you to recall what your Grandma said! I challenge you to read this book with your ears wide open and your heart too. What I share in this book, should be received as if someone is giving you flowers; except these flowers will not die in a few days. Keep this book near you for a quick daily reference. I wrote the way I received from Grandma; with love, gentleness, plainly, and from the heart. Join me as I reminisce about the flowers that my Grandma shared with me. Some of you may have heard what Grandma said so use this as a keepsake to pass down to your children, and children's children.

Grandma

As I sit here with a feeling in me, searching for words to write, wishing I could say that I remember each day that my Grandma said the words I'm about to share. Whoa! I'm going blank. I'm being flooded with emotions. I'm crying now. Okay Sonya look up. Looking up I began to feel better. I see the goodness of what Grandma has taught. Don't brag. Don't hurt others because if you do, expect your feelings to be hurt. I hear you Grandma. I can "smell" where you are coming from. Prayer does change things. Thanks be to God

I Hear You

Breathing, I hear you
As I open my eyes, I hear you
Being Thankful, I hear you
Speaking, I hear you
Cleaning, I hear you
Cooking, I hear you
Singing, I hear you
Sitting, I hear you
Standing, I hear you
Kneeling, I hear you
Eyes closed, I hear you
Unfolding like a blooming flower within me, I hear you

By: Sonya JW Lunsford

Dear Grandma,

I remember you Grandma! Grandma you held me close when you held my hand no matter who could see; walking across a busy street, up and down the church aisles, during the family dinners prior to pulling names and numbers to give out your gifts to everyone attending the gathering and those family members who could not attend. Grandma you knew every member of your family are winners and therefore, you allowed everyone to win. At first I did not understand why me however, as each day goes by, I understand what God allowed you to see in me. One of the lessons you taught me is that I do not need a crowd, to do what God has for me, I only need Christ Jesus, who is my way maker, because God is Love! Thank you Grandmother for allowing your light of LOVE to shine on me and now through me. I miss the feel of your hand but the feel of your peace is still here.

Love Continually Your Granddaughter

Prophetess Sonya JW Lunsford,

P.S. My Grandma always hold my hand...

Better Outcome

A Hard Head Makes
A Sore Butt

At first listen my mind saw a difficult person suffering.

The meaning is just that. Being difficult will cause pain,

either to you and someone else. In a child a difficult

personality will cause those who instruct them to give up on

teaching them and label them as not able to learn or placed

on some sort of punishment. As a parent, difficult children

will be disciplined more than those who cooperate. In the Justice system those who do not follow the rules of law are tossed into solitary confinement; a form of punishment through isolation. Often time than less, time does not permit patience to have its way with a difficult person. When a task is due time is not on your side. You can become nervous and even stressed.

Being in tune with the environment cause for a peaceful existence. Pharaoh from the Bible heart was harden by The Lord. "And the LORD said unto Moses, When thou goest to return into Egypt, see that thou do all those wonders before Pharaoh, which I have put in thine hand: but I will harden his heart, that he shall not let the people go" (Exodus. 4:21 King James Version), Disciplining a hard headed child makes for a sore butt, or pain to someone, even themselves. Pharaoh loss not only his first born but the first born of thousands who followed him. Understanding includes wisdom. Wisdom will aid in choices. The better the choices the better the outcome. Don't get stuck on a good idea that does not produce. Understand the lack of production for what it came to tell you

---

Did You Pray?

Grandma is a prayer warrior. If ever you had a need, and called Grandma, she will hear your plight, then ask did you pray. Right before, you might think, Grandma is about to give me what I want. Oh but no. Grandma's, did you pray, or have you prayed, question was not the answer. Now that I recall, most of these conversations where over the phone. My mouth flew open, to signify my shock, and confusion. Imaging calling your Grandma and she answers with all the care of sweet Grandma. She listen to every word, careful not to interrupt. Finally you say, Grandma, what should I do. Did you pray? I answer, yes or no. Either answer lead to Grandma praying for me and with me. I did not enjoy being asked this question. I did not like it mainly because it questioned my prayer life. As I matured, I know that question held more value than the help I expected from Grandma. I did not like hearing the question, but it was what I needed. Grandma knows the answer and she also know who holds the answers. Even if I prayed, I evidently did not hear the answer. Had I heard the answer, I would not be asking Grandma. Wisdom is the best teacher, though some prefer experience first.

Do What Your Momma Say

"My son, keep your father's command and do not forsake your mother's teaching" (Proverbs 6:20 King James Version). Mother knows best, is what come to mind. I know not all who give birth are mothers but surely many are. That Mother who cares for you, you should obey, by doing what she say.

Don't Like The Way
Your Baby Looks

Sometimes when we are first time mothers, and see our baby for the first time, what we see does not make us smile; it is not a good look. The shape of the baby's head can scare you at first sight. The baby's skin sometimes is not smooth. Plus the baby might look like someone totally different than you thought. I was one of those mothers and yes, Grandma said, keep oiling, and praying, things will get better. I did the oiling and praying. Yes! Things did get better. That post-partum is real. It is best we save all our comments. What comes out sometimes is hurtful. Nerves are on edge. Your body is simply a strange creature. We had months to prepare for our babies, and now the baby is out. Separate from us. The emotions are changing as we breathe in and out. God is good and God is great! Beautiful baby blossomed. Thanks Grandma!

God Did It For Me
He'll Do It For You

God is not a respecter of person. As spoken in The
Book of Acts of the Bible "Then Peter began to speak: "I
now realize how true it is that God does not show
favoritism" (New International Version Acts. 10:34). God
loves us all. God loves each of us and all the same.
What we do with that love shows how we love God or if
we love God. Looking at what others have, wishing we
had it too or better than them, is a sure way we miss the
greatness God planned for us. We must look to God for
what God has for each of us. Each of our greatness is
equal in God's sight. Therefore, God's plan for us has
been equally planned. "This mystery is that through the
gospel the Gentiles are heirs together with Israel,
members together of one body, and sharers together in
the promise in Christ Jesus."

(Ephesians 3:6 New International Version)

I Surrender All

I surrender all was what I call my Grandma's Solo! Grandma would sing this song all the way to the box called Tithe. The Tithe box was positioned front and center of the Church. Before entering the pulpit, you would pass the Tithe box. The musician would strike the keys and after the first stanza of music was played the church would unite in song, singing, I Surrender All. However when it came to the chorus part my Grandma would hit a high note and that began her solo. All the same, my ears could only hear Grandma's voice. The strength and determination she had in giving was satisfying to my heart's soul. She would get up and walk as she sang, down toward the box called Tithe. Once she reached it, Grandma placed her tithe through the opening in the top. Grandma would slowly return to her seat and the song would end always in a timely fashion.

As I became an adult My Grandma's legs did not move as swiftly. She would ask me to take her tithe down. Nevertheless, Grandma would always sing her solo I Surrender All, as I proceeded. I learned we might get weary in these bodies but our will can remain strong. Grandma was teaching us, giving takes all. She also knew, giving your all to God, would answer all other needs. "Love the LORD your God with all your heart and with all your soul and with all your strength" (Deuteronomy 6:5 New International Version)

Lead By Example

One of my first memories of Grandma was her showing me gymnastics. Here's what happened: Grandma watched us play. We, the children, were in her back yard. She saw the older children trying but failing to complete a cartwheel. The older children were really trying and I was watching per their body language instructions; "stay out of the way or you will get hurt".

Their legs were swinging all kinds of ways, as they threw

themselves toward the ground. I decided to watch from

the safe haven of the back porch. "No feet kicking me in

the face", I thought. Grandma appeared in the back

door. "I'll show you how to do a cartwheel", Grandma

said. I remember thinking, cartwheel? Grandma

removed her apron and laid it ever so carefully across

the chair situated on the porch near where I stood. As

she approached the older children, Grandma moved her

arms in and out signaling them to give her more space.

To the side the children went. Then up went Grandma's

hands, her arms out stretched. Then down to the ground

they went. Up went her feet! Grandma is upside down!

"Her Hands are where her feet once were", I thought.

But quick as her hands touch the ground, they were

back up again. Grandma said, "That's how it is done".

"I'm 50 years old; you can do it if I can". My eyes must

have been as wide as they could get and my smile too! I

was very proud of my Grandma. She was leading by being an example. I recall stepping off the porch then unto the yard, determined not to fail in completing a cartwheel. I succeeded of course and went on to teach myself the other gymnastic positions. All I needed was the "G", encyclopedia and an open space.

Never Discipline The Child In Front Of The Parent

The truth be told no parent enjoys hearing are seeing their child disciplined by others. The child feels free and happier to see the parent and may behave much differently. This different behavior might seem out of order, but do not discipline the child, if needed the parent is present and is now the lead adult. Allow the parent the space to handle the situation if any occurs. This method is used for good news too. When the parent enters if the child wants to share a good experience, allow the child to speak while you observe. This creates an opportunity for you to witness how the child articulates the day. The conversation is a great tool for future corrections if needed in your environment or what you can continue offering as a good service to the child. If the child swings from the staircase or jump on furniture in the present of the parent allow it to happen. If the parent does not administer discipline in front of you that is okay, remember, you are not the lead adult at this time. The rules of your home are there and should have been articulated to both parent and child, but if rules are broken during this transfer of child to parent, allow. Why not discipline when parent is present, it also prolongs the transfer. Allow the bouncing happy or sad child to leave in peace.

No Such Thing As A Child Having A Child

Grandma said, "God is in control". There are certain things that have not changed. Girls come on their period[1] and boys begin to shoot- off[2]. Once that girl starts menstruating she is no longer a child. She is in womanhood that makes her a woman. Likewise, when a boy starts ejaculating, he is in manhood. He is a man. If ever they meet, if it's the Lord's Will, they will get pregnant. All this children having children information is wrong, Grandma said. God made the plan for a girl to turn into a woman and a boy to turn into a man. The age when this happens occurs at different times of life, but it does occur at the appropriate time. A child cannot have a child. Just because she or he are young does not a child make them, if they are in womanhood and manhood, then they are no longer a child. I know the law says we are under age, but remember that is man's law. Not God's Law. So stop beating up on the young people when they become pregnant. Sure they are young and

---

[1] Period - female menstruation
[2] Shoot-off here indicate male ejaculation

perhaps inexperienced, but we all are lacking in some way or another. God fixed that.

We Must Change Because God Cannot Use Us The Way We Are

Doing things the way you want to do them sounds great, but we all must change. Change is good when wisdom is the guide. Our life is to be used for the better good. Sometimes we get caught up starring in our own movie. However, when we mature in the Lord, the truth comes and resides in us as a measuring stick and change happens. Yes, change from our way to a better way. God can use us for good, or for what appears bad, only pray for the use of being good. Joseph spoke of such happenings. "You intended to harm me, but God intended it for good to accomplish what is now being done, the saving of many lives" (Genesis 20:50 New International Version) Joseph's brothers did what is considered a bad thing towards Joseph, however, God had their badness in the plan to bring about good. When we seek to do things, God's way the plan might appear bad or filled with lack, but hold on to God's unchanging hand and your faith will remove all doubt and replace it with more faith. Your faith will show forth as truth and the truth will never change. On the other hand truth will lead us to change. Knowing our truth is not what we have decided, but what God has said is our truth. There is a plan for our life. Seek the plan in the Word of God and you and I will find our truth. When we know our truth, change is happening and God can use us now! We will have something to say. Testify!

When You Send Children Out To Play, You Must Watch

This statement had a powerful impact in my life. I enjoyed having all the family children around me. Seeing their smiles and knowing they were safe because I was watching and listening. I would interject only if confusion started if not before. I would become mediator. But if questions continued without understanding on the children part, I would have sit down time. Sit down time included talking to one another and sharing the thoughts of what caused the confusion. Play would continue after peace ensued. Play time is when most bullies are made. Bullies who once were nice children with bad ideas have the opportunity to put into play their thoughts, just to see if it works. To keep all children healthy and happy adults must be involved. Adults who will not take sides but offer answers to make smiles come on each child involved face. They all are very important little people. Sometimes adults leave to handle other business like dish washing or watching TV while children play, but this is discouraged. Please be ever present while children play. Know your presence is needed until each child is able to do what you do; play fairly. When bad situations arise, most adults miss their onset. An adult being present should lessen bad situations. The questions must be asked and answered of each child. Try not to omit an involved child. Every child's voice should be heard. Adults who involve themselves make children happier even if the child complains. Complaining is part of being a child. Watch and listen then do something if necessary.

You Have To Crawl Before You Walk

I shared with Grandma about a baby walking but I did not see the baby crawl. Grandma said, "you have to crawl before you walk." "But Grandma", I said, "this baby stood up and started walking." Grandma said, "I have known people who walked before they crawled and before they left this world they crawled." Wow Grandma! "Yes", she continued, "there is an order to doing things. "We are set to do them all." You may skip, but you still have to complete that task you skipped. It is better to crawl while you are a baby than to crawl as an adult. Crawling is for a short span, walking is for the rest of your life. If you crawl as a baby you will not have to crawl as an adult. I took what Grandma said to life. Do not try to skip the process, go through the process. Step by step. Make sure to compete each task. Mastering each task is necessary. Don't be in such a hurry to get grown enjoy being a child. Do not rush

2

Considering Others First

Give Me My Flowers
While I Am Alive

I wanted the flowers placed before each patch of

wisdom Grandma said, because each word Grandma

said grew in my heart. When I grew up, I began to hear

people say, give me my flowers while I can smell them. I

would think, that's not what my Grandma said to me

when I was a child. She said give me flowers while I am alive. I asked Grandma about this difference in the sayings and Grandma told her story of how she lost her sense of smell as a young person. I remember thinking Grandma can't smell! An adult now, I wondered, how did Grandma know we needed baths? Thinking back to my child hood, Grandma would instruct us to bathe. I did not grasp she knew when we came from outside – playtime- we needed bathing. She told me I needed a bath. I laughed and thought of the words Grandma said. Grandma never lied. She never said she smelled me. She said, "you need a bath." SMH[3] I smiled. I said Grandma I love you! This is why Grandma said give me my flowers while I am alive instead of while I can smell them.

---

[3] SMH is the acronym for 'shaking my head'.

If You Don't Have Something Nice To Say, Don't Say

Many of us will say we have heard about this saying. But when I heard it, it was from Grandma. We are quick to say we know, but what you know is what you show. If the statement, If you don't have something nice to say, don't say nothing, would be applied our world would be a better place if not much quieter. Think about that joke that comes at the expense of someone else. Even try to stop talking about yourself negatively. Our emotional environment would blossom beautiful flowers instead of the sometimes sticky briars and thorns. Thorns like the ones Jesus' crown was fashion out of. If we could see the blood dripping from the damage we actually cause from the words that are not good to say toward one another, maybe we would reconsider who we really believe in. Who we really represent. Are there any boundaries? There are people who say nothing is off limit. You Tube videos that simulate comedic stances. Leaving hurt emotions all over the place. When some are called on to explain why, they say it's funny. Or they blame the subject of their comedy, by saying keep your business to yourself if you don't want to be talked about. We who are responsible for taking up the cross must know the cross includes wisdom. Wisdom shows you the outcome of your words and deeds. Wisdom calls you to be conscience and responsible for the state of mind you leave a person in. Wisdom has no age limit, sexism, racism or classism. If we really want the world, environment, the youth to respect, we who know better must be seen doing better, and not just financially. Words do hurt, kill, and destroy. Words can give life, liberty, happiness. Which do you prefer to be the handler of? Remember we reap what we sow.

Keep Living

Grandma said this to those who could not believe. For example if someone was trying to explain their situation to others, but to no avail, Grandma would say, keep living, life has a way of showing us just what is and is not. She also would say, "if you live long enough you will understand." But you must keep living! Grandma this is a good way to teach empathy, I thought. Then I said it out loud. Grandma this helps us understand one another. It also keeps us from judging. Life is a good teacher however, life is not always kind, or easy going. It also meant if the person is deceitful the truth would soon be found. I learned how to believe and let be.

When You Eat In Front Of Others, Offer Them Some; Share

When I first heard Grandma say, don't eat in front of others unless you have enough to share, she was talking to someone else. I took that bit of wisdom and ran with it.

When I was a child I shared to a fault so some would

say, but as an adult I measure my sharing by trying the

spirit by the spirit. If I did not have enough to share I kept

it until I was by myself. Grandma being wise understood

somedays people would leave home without eating.

Somedays there was no food to eat. Therefore,

Grandma prepared snacks. She would use plastic

sandwich bags. In each bag several goodies to keep the

children quiet in church, on the bus, or around the

neighborhood until parents returned home. Grandma

always fed the hungry and gave to the needy. She

always had some treats in her bag. Grandma did not

need special occasions to bring gifts, she is a gift. Each

week she prepared Sunday giveaways. She gave to the

children and adults. She would give out immediately

after service. Some complained about the paper

wrappers left near or in the church from those whom she

gave to, this almost caused her not to give. But because

this is a part of Grandma's Ministry, God guided her in teaching others not to litter. When God gives you a task, the way is already made. When Grandma's legs did not work well, she would ask me to pass the gifts around. But believe me she asked others too. When she realized she was missing some church goers. She had us place her in a chair near the entrance of the Church as she touched all who desired to receive with her gift giving ministry. "Do not neglect to do good and to share what you have, for such sacrifices are pleasing to God" (Hebrews 13:16 English Standard Version)

3.

Family Ties

A Family That Prays Together

Stays Together

This one seemed plain to understand. My Grandma

made many Biblical sounding statements. I went

searching for this in the Bible and could not find it. What I

found is more. Yes, more understanding that I thought I

would. God used Grandma to cause me to study. While

studying the Bible I researched the Words and their meaning was part of my findings. Whenever a group of people did anything together in the name of Jesus, he promised to be there. He promised to give them anything, if they could agree. Praying together builds a family. Coming together makes a group. Understanding each other's needs enough to agree, is power. Such power like this is missed by most. This gift is specifically for those who have eyes to see and ears to hear. Touching an agreeing is not easy. However, with God agreeing is possible. Moreover, yes, necessary to receive heavenly results on earth, "for where two or three are gathered together in my name, there am I in the midst of them" (Matthew 18:20 King James Version) "Again I say unto you, That if two of you shall agree on earth as touching anything that they shall ask, it shall be done for them of my Father which is in heaven" Matthew 18:19 (King James Version) Grandma wanted her family to do what it took to come together; to mature in love. Grandma said praying together will make us a better family. Seeking the righteousness of God will bring a family together. When there are some who do not want to seek God, but pretend, the family will be at war. A warring family is not at peace. The children will not be at peace. The relationships will not be at peace. The head of each family must exemplify prayer as a need to succeed. Godly success will bring families together not tear them apart. Godly success will cause each member of the family to look at themselves for solutions to the family problems. Simply put, when you are truly happy you want to make sure others are happy too. When true happiness happens, the joy comes from within. Joy is not given by mankind, but by God. Joy fills your heart. A heart full of joy has no room for jealousy, or any other ill behaviors. So when the family members are not together, true joy is absent and ill fillings are present. If you want to judge, judge how your children are relating to life. Judge how they are related to those in their life. How do they treat others? Knowing what joy is through the giving of Godly love, will guide us all to become a family that prays together. We must know the time is now to pray. The moment is now! Each member must know the responsibility is theirs. Each family member must come to realize, being the oldest does not make you right or wrong, good or bad. God is good all by God's self. God is just. God is the true and every man/woman is a lie. Look to each other in trueness. Forgive yourself and you can show forgiveness toward your other family members. Talking a good game is not needed. Making others think your family is together when they really are not, is a lie. And it only serves to prolong the praying together as a family. Are you ready to do the work of Godly Love? God did what was necessary to bring his family together and yes, it included praying. What prayer and deed can you see yourself doing to bring your family together?

My Prayer/ Deed

Children Might Hear What You Say But They Do What You Do

Too many times adults offer unsolicited advice. It's for your own good, they say. Don't do like I did. Adults want children to do better than they did. Adults ask children to overcome faults they could not overcome. The truth; in these situations, children listen to what adults say, but do what they see adults do. Actions speak louder than words comes to mind. I get it some adults give their life as a testimony. But this is not just about a living testimony; it is about not being a hypocrite. Yes, expecting others to do better than you did against the same stumbling blocks, while you only offer advice is hypocritical and a step close to judging. Adults should strive to improve on what they consider "failing", in the presence of children. Showing them the finish product does not teach children problem solving techniques. Showing the end and never the go through is falsity. It confuses children. Adults stand the chance of pushing the children further toward the

opposite of their success. The child only sees your

success and never your failing, will think you are perfect

and they could never live up to that perfection. Flaws are

needed. On the other hand if all you show children are

your failings, it does not matter how you explain that they

should go the other way, the child will follow closely

behind, either emotionally or physically. Even God used

the life of Jesus as an example. God wanted to show us a

perfect life. A life of perfection. Sometimes perfection

shows up as failings, or unsuccessful. God knew what we

needed and therefore sent Jesus to show us what God

meant. Too many times adults wonder why children

stumble. Adults all over raising children or teaching

children, say I told you that would not work, or that was

not a good idea, or do not do that. Children who see

adult's words match their actions, repeat the actions

gladly. But let one be missing and a different outcome will

occur. I hope this helps someone. I hope some adult

decides to provoke the children around them to greatness, through clear cut examples. Children listening to what is said, but do what they see as examples from their environment. If you do not want your business getting out watch what you do in front of the children. Even if you enjoy a smoke, don't smoke in front of your children, unless this is what you want your children to become; a smoker. Remember even if you survived the drug use, drinking, multiple sex partners, or bad relationships, does not cause your children to get over them, or survive. Adults who say they want the best for their children will find these words gratifying and strive toward showing a better side of wisdom in front of the children. Adults who find these words offensive, have decided, their children are not worth it and neither are their grandchildren.

Two Grandmas

I am one of those people who had two Grandmas as I grew to become an adult. My Mother's Mother and my Father's Mother. I was raised calling one Grandma and the other Big Momma; but knowing they both are my Grandma. I see them the same. They are needed. They can cook. They are beautiful! They love God. They are Mothers. They are determined to be a positive influence in my life. They are not perfect, but they are all mine! Well, except for the other children that kept calling them Grandma or Big Momma. You know like my siblings and the children of my aunts and uncles. Go figure! LOL![4] Yes they eventually were a part of teaching me how to share. I came to know them both as "Gifts from God".

---

[4] LOL is an acronym for 'laugh out loud'

You Should Have
Named Her Sandra

All I remember is Grandma saying Sonja come here.
I knew it was me she was calling. My Mother's name
happen to be Sandra. Grandma advised her to name me
Sandra. I asked Mother why she named me Sonya
instead of Sandra. "I decided to find a name close to the
meaning of my name and that's how I found the name
Sonya," Mother said. Grandma seemed to not agree with
this decision and called me Sonja every time. On every
Birthday Card she wrote Sonja. All my life Sonja was my
name Grandma's way of compromising I guess. Sonya
and Sandra together. Grandma's sister and brothers
called me Sonja too. I guess when they asked what I
was named, Grandma's voice was loudest. Because on
every Birthday Card from her siblings Happy Birthday
Sonja was written. My name appeared on many Church
Bulletins and as guest speakers on programs. My

mother named me Sonya, yet my Grandma and her siblings still call me and spell my name, Sonja. LOL! What can you do but love it all!

4

Good Times

Grandma Has Super Powers

Another memory of Grandma caused me to realize

Grandmas are Mothers of parents. I put two and two

together and concluded, Parents have Mothers too! Big

Momma is Daddy's Mother. Grandma is Mommies

Mother. Daddy has to do what Big Momma tells him like

I have to do what he tells me. I was going to use this

newly discovered knowledge to my full advantage. I

began to notice how Dad loved his Mother. How she

called his name and he came quickly. Yep! She's his

Mother. One day an incident occurred at home and I was

punished. I didn't mind being punished if I deserved it.

But this particular time I felt the punishment did not fit;

let's be honest, what child does. Moving right ahead with

the story, I took my punishment, I also waited until the

day we would visit Big Momma's house. The day finally

came. I waiting for the perfect time before approaching

Big Momma. All I could think of is, "I'm telling on Daddy

today". There she is. She is alone. No witnesses. As

she stood in the kitchen, I approached her with my head

hung low. "Big Momma", I called out to her. "Yes baby",

she said. Then out came the whole detailed incident.

Her eyes widen as she called my Daddy to her side. She

quietly spoke to him, with me by her side. Daddy might

have thought this was not a nice time, but for me it had

turned into the best day ever. I felt so safe. I felt relieved.

I felt loved. My Big Momma is my hero! She has a super

power. Grandmas are the best! I love her! My heart was

full of joy! I paused for a moment and thought, I wonder if I will be punished for this. Then immediately I got happy! Inside my hands were stretched high up and I was jumping up and down! Singing Super Powers! Super Powers! Grandma have super powers! But on the outside, I stayed by Grandmas side for as long as I could, just to be safe. My Daddy got the message and so did I. Love you Daddy! It's good to have a Daddy and even better to have a Grandma. Grandmas have Super Powers! Well, at least mine do!

Organ Play

Grandma had this organ and she could play it too! These visits are getting better and better! Big Momma is it alright if I play the organ? Can you play? I can try! I then thought, I can play clarinet, maybe the notes are similar. Okay go ahead, play, Grandma said. I sat at the huge organ and opened the Hymnal. Great there are notes! I search for an easy tune. I found one! I began to play slowly. One note at a time listening to hear if I was making the music like the adults did. I was so happy. It did not matter if it sounded good or not. I'm happy! I'm happy! Grandma eventually gave me that organ as part of her Will; even though she gave it to me while she is alive. She said I'm not waiting, I want you to have this organ so I'm giving it to you now, Sonya! Do you want it? YES! Grandma gave me flowers while she yet lives.

Ride Me Till I Sweat

One of Grandma's favorite things to do was going riding. She did not care where she sat, front, back, near the door, or in the middle. Grandma was always satisfied just to be riding. It seemed to ease her-giving her peace. I often would take Grandma with me. I would take her shopping. Taking my Grandmothers shoe shopping became our thing to do. Shopping for shoes, window shopping, and a nice meal of Grandma's choice, then back home. Satisfied until we went again. I took each of my Grandmas shopping on their own day, never together. It was my treat and a blessing from God that I had two Grandmothers and the finances to splurge on them every now and then. The shoe choice is always theirs. My Grandmas had just about everything they could want. They would like the same brand of shoe, but not the same style. I really enjoyed the difference.

On several occasions, I got lost. There's this one time in particular, I rode until we saw no street lights. Even the road became gravel. Grandma was sitting quietly all the time knowing I am lost. I would remain cool and calm. But Grandma knew I was lost. The lights gone and the road is gone. LOL! Grandma asked," baby are you lost." I wanted to burst out laughing! But I simply answered, yes Grandma, I'm lost". Grandma did not get upset, she said, I'm okay, just ride me till I sweat! Thinking of that moment days, months, and now years later, I can't help but laugh and shake my head. I turned around and I drove back the way I came. We never made it to where we planned to go that day. But we always had that lost episode as a good memory and we laughed through the years remembering it.

Singing Me To Peace

I often sat and talked with my Grandma and she prayed a lot. Mostly for her family. Grandma said, God promised her that He would save her whole household. Grandma lived by faith. God did not promise her perfection, God promised her salvation. That was good enough for Grandma. Grandma would sing and I would join in as best I could. Too often I got lost in her voice. I would close my eyes and sway my head back and forth to the rhythm of the song. I was satisfied just to hear her sing. Very peaceful sitting and listening to Grandma sing. Singing the praises of God. Singing about how she felt about God. Grandma was teaching me how and why to praise God! My parents would sing and it made me very happy. Dad and his brothers would sing, I knew singing would be my ability too! Oh how they would harmonized. They can sang, I'd say! But I digress. Okay one more digression, I asked my Uncles to sing at my wedding, and they all did. Yay! Back to Grandma now.

Take Me Where The Happenings Are

Grandma said with a snap in her step. Take me where the happenings are! She knew this would get a laugh from me. I asked, "What are the happenings?" Grandma said, the place where the goings on are. Thinking with a tilt of my head, goings on. Grandma saw my puzzled expression then she further explained. There are places we go to dance, sing, and talk or simply laugh at a good joke. Shopping downtown. Where there is people handling business. The happenings! Some go to clubs to dance and meet others. Sitting out on the porch or park bench watching as people walk by. Down town to social clubs.

Grandma wanted a little action. Grandma and I went

driving. I drove her where she wanted to go. Sightseeing is

what it turns out she needed. What Grandma called the

happenings I called seeing the sights.

5

God in It

God Don't Like ugly And
He Isn't To Keen On Pretty!

This was always said with a chuckle of a laugh by

Grandma to me. Then she would get serious as she

explained. It was to show behavior. Being not nice is

ugly even if you think you are pretty. God sees all and

knows all. He is El Roi, The God Who Sees. It is better

to attempt good deeds no matter how you look! Thinking

you are better than others in the sight of God is ugly.

When we think that way our behavior reveals how far we

are from God. When we say we are good yet our actions

are hurtful, sometimes, if not all of the times we are

revealing what is actually in our hearts. Our action must

match our words and our spirit must match God's Spirit.

"The good person out of the good treasure of his heart

produces good, and the evil person out of his evil

treasure produces evil, for out of the abundance of the

heart his mouth speaks" (Luke 6:45 English Standard

Version)

God Is Love

Grandma was Superintendent of Sunday School.

Later I learned this was a covenant position. I remember

when Grandma affixed GOD IS LOVE to the church

walls; the walls of the Sunday school. Some wondered

why. Nevertheless, Grandma is a born teacher and is on

her God given mission. These words have been engraved over and over in Bibles and sold all over the world! "He that loveth not knoweth not God; for God is love" (1John 4:8 King James Version) Teach Grandma teach! I recall the words Grandma put up on the walls being red, then metallic gold, then red again. I'm sure God is still loving and the words should be written in the hearts of all who know Grandma. So many talk about love. Marriages are formed because we say we are in love. God is love. The love is thrown around like air. When we use the word love, it should remind us of God. Love is God. When we marry because we are in love, then it goes to understand we are in God. Oh, not the same you say. Well, I beg to differ. God is passion. God is good, God is love. The work God did on the cross through the embodiment of Jesus the Christ, is God's passion. Jesus said none is good except the father who is God the father. Enough said. Think, pray to God about this love, you are in before the marriage, so that the marriage will keep. Seek wise counsel not just someone who will agree to your terms. God is love and those who love must love as God loves us.

God Takes Care Of
Old Folks And Children

This statement left me thinking, am I the Child since I'm not yet old. Okay, God where do I fit in. I'm the Child. Being young we often behave foolishly. And yes, we blame it on:

1. Being a child
2. I did not know
3. Nobody taught me that

What Grandma said helped me understand, God takes care of us all. This statement Grandma said included us all. Of course nobody considered finding themselves as immature. But let's be honest, nobody is looking. We have exhibited some foolish behaviors. When we do not know better, God has our back. When we can't do any better, God has our back. Does any of us fit in either category? I do. What about you? The Old Folk part is the rest. Grandma considered Old Folk as having had the opportunity more than others to exhibit wisdom instead of childish behavior. However wisdom has taught me that getting older does not make one wise. I've seen some Old Folk behave foolishly. Either case rest assured God has our back. God is looking out for our best. Now if only we all believed and got under that covenant of forgive and let go. Because, we only show what we know; childlike or old folk.

Grandma The Encourager

I can still see Grandma as she stood in the kitchen cooking and sharing her wisdom. I remember as she sat on the sofa looking through photo albums, pointing to photos and sharing their memories. I recall when Grandma walked through the church praying, cleaning, and teaching me about family coming together in the

Lord, in a place prepared for their inheritage. Even, as she lay on her bed tired from her day, Grandma encouraged me. Yes, Grandma said a lot to me. She was encouraging me. Many times I thought she was just being Grandma. Sitting here praying and allowing the Spirit of God to guide me, I can really hear what Grandma said to me. Sonya come help me with these numbers for the family gift drawing. Will you make me some Bookmarkers that say, Happy Valentine Day, and Happy Mother's Day. Sonya will you have a little prayer with me. Sonya make sure you check that they give you the correct number. Sonya did you do my stickers yet? Sonya let the teacher teach. Go into the pulpit and do what God said. Hearing these words come from Grandma resonated in my soul. Sonya you know who you are, and you know what you must do. You are the one Sonya, as she took my hand and squeezed gently. Remember Sonya if people do not choose you, don't worry, because God already has. I heard you Grandma. I hear you!

Please Forgive Me

This is what Grandma would ask us to repeat after each prayer she lead. In the name of Jesus, Lord please forgive me for the things, that I did, said, and thought wrong, and I did not know any better. Now Lord, please forgive me for the things I did, said, and thought wrong, and I did know better. Please forgive me Lord, because I do realize, I am wrong, some of the time, most of the time, if not all of the time. Please forgive me. Amen! Now turn to one another and ask, Will you forgive me? Then respond to one another in love. Now say, thank You God with a hug!

Study The Red Words

When I started studying the Bible, Grandma advised me to study all what illustrated what Jesus said. Okay, this is how she did it. One day Grandma pulled me to the side and whispered ever so discreetly to me, I found out if you read the red words, you will know the whole understanding of the Bible. I followed Grandmas advice. Yes! Now I share that same advice. I tested that theory and to this day, the answer to Bible questions come to me even if I have not actually read the words. The Red Words are powerful and you can live your life in peace once you receive what they have to say. I have seen Bibles with Red Letters even in the Old Testament. But at the time Grandma said read the red words, I only knew of the red being in the New Testament. Understanding the Bible is filled with wisdom, but the red letters are the best for me.

The Lord's Prayer

After this manner therefore pray ye: Our Father which art in heaven, Hallowed be thy name Thy kingdom come, Thy will be done in earth, as it is in heaven. Give us this day our daily bread. And forgive us our debts, as we forgive our debtors. And lead us not into temptation, but deliver us from evil: For thine is the kingdom, and the power, and the glory, forever" (Matthew 6:9-13 King James Version) Always pray In Jesus name Amen!

Grandma would notice how many times the Lord's Prayer was prayed during her day. Once during Church Service, Grandma said, "Sonya, The Lord's Prayers' was prayed 5 times today." She began to count with her fingers, first this morning during Sunday school at the end of the lesson. Second, when we made the Sunday School circle at the end. Third, the Choir prayed it, before coming out. Fourth, after the Altar Call. And fifth,

after Holy Communion. 5 times! Five is the number for

grace!

The Spirit Doesn't Dwell
With You Always

The Spirit of God, Grandma said, gives us life and

strength and there are times the Spirit has to lift from us.

Lifting from us does not mean God has left us. God is

always near. God promised, and it is written throughout

the Bible, God will never leave or forsake us. However,

the flesh, which is our body, the skin we live in, becomes

tired which is an indication of lack. The lack feels

tiresome and we think rest is needed. We get tired

sometimes. We are filled. We get empty. We need

refilling. That feeling of needing refilling is when the

Spirit has gone from us. This is not a bad thing. The

Spirit lifting from us, need to happen. We would not

sleep if the Spirit does not lift from us. The Spirit has to lift from us so we can rest. When we are in the middle of a task and get weary, faint is near, we call on the Spirit of God, through the Word of God and the Spirit comes and restores us. Really, to rest, we must ask for help. Use the Word of God as our catalyst. The Word of God will speak to the Spirit on our behalf. "The word of God is alive and active, sharper than any double-edged sword. It cuts all the way through, to where soul and spirit meet, to where joints and marrow come together. It judges the desires and thoughts of the heart." (Hebrews 4:12 Good News Translation).

When death is near our spirit is leaving us preparing to exit our body. When the spirit is absent from the body the body is dead. We only live here for a few years and then we move from these bodies. The Spirit that comes from God our creator has to return to God. The body must return to the earth form. i.e. dust. "Our soul parish. His spirit departs, he returns to the earth; in that very day his thoughts perish" We all are spirits that live in a body and possess souls. (Psalms 146: 4 New International

Version) "I pray God your

whole spirit and soul and body be preserved blameless

unto the coming of our Lord Jesus Christ"

(1 Thessalonians 5:23 New International Version)

The Spirit Is Willing
But The Flesh Is Weak

I have experienced this many times. Often I wanted,

even felt I wanted to do an act, but I could not. I had the

will to do but not the strength. Spiritually I felt like

superwoman but in this little body, weak. I was in some

ways like the disciples. Jesus asked them watch and

pray. However their interpretation of watch and pray

could not measure to Jesus' needs. They went to sleep

each time he asked it of them. Jesus eventually said,"

"Keep watching and praying that you may not enter into

temptation; the spirit is willing, but the flesh is weak."

(Matthew 26:41 New American Standard Bible). I'm sure

like I feel at times, the disciples did not want to fail Jesus. They truly desired to stay awake. Jesus felt weak in his body, at this hour and wanted them to help him. But I know God the father was teaching another lesson; depend only on me. Jesus learned a lesson and taught one too! Jesus was all powerful and weak at the same time. The Will[5] to do the Will he was sent here to fulfill, overcame him in the form of grief. He wanted an escape. But God the Father being true to His Word, already knew this would come to Jesus and one day to us. God the father used Jesus as the perfect example. When we are weak it does not mean we are not spiritually strong. Our weakness is because of the flesh; these bodies. In spirit Jesus was strong- even a God but in the flesh weak and subject to all the humanly frailties. I hope this helps you in understanding, we should not be hard on ourselves when it appear as though we are coming up short.

---

[5] Will with the uppercase W, indicates God's Will

There Go I Save For
The Grace Of God

So grace is favor, "unmerited favor." Grace is,

therefore, God's unmerited favor - His goodness toward

those who have no claim on, nor reason to expect, divine

favor. The principal manifestation of God's grace has been

in the form of a gift. God gifted us with His Grace. Even

when we appear to suffer God's grace is at hand. Seeing

a woman walk by who appeared homeless or perhaps on

drugs, Grandma said, "There go I save for the grace of

God". Grandma knew God's Grace saved her from such a

life and handed her the life she lives. God gives to us what

He knows we can handle. God never gives us what we

deserve. That's where His Grace comes in. We should be

thankful, whatever our conditions, because there is always

someone worst, or better. And as for that woman

Grandma said, "God's Grace is sufficient for her too"!

(1Corinthians 15:10 New Living Translation)

There Will Be Times When You Need To Call On The Name Of Jesus But You Will Find It Difficult

Me: Why won't I be able Grandma? Why won't I call on Jesus especially if I need Him?

Grandma: Well we can get in such a way that our mind won't let us. We can get so angry words dare part our lips. We can be so confused in the mind that our thoughts will not tell us, we are worthy to call on the name of Jesus. When you are in that state of mind, the word Jesus won't come.

Me: Grandma how do we get to Jesus from that point?

Grandma: Now what I am telling you is not just for those who do very bad things it is for people who get in any way that separate us from the Spirit of God's peace; When you can't feel hope, when you feel alone, when you feel challenged, when you cannot see a way to the solution. You must close off the thoughts that are causing you anger, and that is causing your mind to wander in places that you ought not to go, telling you all sorts of things against yourself; things that really are thoughts that do not shine you in a good light. Thoughts like, No, never, you think you know everything, you think you are better than we are, no way, you will not make it through, you think that will work. In addition, you are not any good.

Me: Grandma you sound like you are preaching

Grandma: You see, God knows just how much you can bear!

"There hath no temptation taken hold of you but such as is common to man. But God is faithful; He will not suffer you to be tempted beyond that which ye are able to bear, but with the temptation will also make a way to escape, that ye may be able to bear it." (1Corinthians

10:13 New International Version) When you hear any of these thoughts, sit, stand, and stop the rambling of thoughts. Once you have begun to do that, a little ray of light in the form of hope, or clear thought will appear, and a soft, polite voice will say, "It's alright, say Jesus now". In that moment of stillness, you say Jesus. Joy will fill you at that moment. You will immediately say Jesus again, and away the ill spirits will flee! Jesus again and again! Works every time, yes it does. Ha! Ha! (As she, rocked against her bed pillow.)

Me: Wow! (I smiled!)

I knew that was Grandma's way of praising God and saying take that bad spirit back to the dark place it came from in Jesus name!

6

Handling Conflict

*A Good Run Is Better Than
A Bad Stand Any Day!*

Words to live by from the day Grandma said them to

me. I asked Grandma to explain. Grandma said," There

are times when you are in a tight spot. You are angry

perhaps. And you want to fight. But your insides are not in

agreement with you. Maybe the ratio is off. The place is

not feasible. The timing is not good. Maybe you are plain scared. Whatever the circumstances you've gathered yourself enough to know it would be wise to run instead of physically fighting, so that you can live to fight another day. Time came and time went. Situations could at time become rough to handle. Seeing your life or someone else life flash before you are great times to apply, a run is better than a bad stand any day. Running is good. Standing is good too! But the two goods have vast endings! You will need to pick the running and standing times. Some runs are spiritual and some runs are physical. Some stands are spiritual and some stands are physical. Sometimes running will leave you bruised spiritually but not physically. On the other hand, some standing will cause you to feel a physical pain that your spirit will need healing from; you know emotional damage. Hopefully you will allow wisdom to be your friend and aid you in the decisions of when to run in order to stand another day. I recall running and later laughing so hard.

Yes laughing because I was alive to laugh. Gunshots fired, when you are without a gun is not the time to stand unless the standing you do is praying. If you are in a relationship, being abused, run. Run until you can stand and laugh! If it is not funny yet! Keep running!

A Little Bird Told Me

This is what Grandma said when she knew a secret about you or someone else. The start of a conversation, a question and answers always would follower.

Sometimes You Must Give Up Your Right For Someone Else Wrong

Again I hear words coming out of Grandma's mouth, words that were not easy to hear. Why should I give up my right for someone else's wrong? Sometimes situations cause for diplomacy. I can think of several; however I'll only share two portrayals affect.

Situation #1:

Let us say you are standing or walking when approached by someone who politely says, "Good evening may I have your purse?" You look into the eyes of this person because it's as if they know you, but they do not! Next, you look into their eyes to see if they are serious and yes, they are! They do not move and you notice a gun pointing. This person has approached you ever so politely, garnishing a gun asking for your purse. That's not right and surely, this person is wrong. But guess what, you give up that bag keeping your rights to yourself. Thinking: Sometimes you must give up your right for someone else's wrong! Knowing you have the right to walk out of a boutique to your vehicle did not stop the robber. In fact, it gave him the purpose of robbing you. Being on the side of right does not negate you being wronged.

Situation #2:

Having a discussion with someone, you respect. You've been in each other's lives for years. There have been good times and bad times, tears and cheers. Life has been unfolding and you and this person have been in it together. But now a disagreement is happening. You know you are right. You presented evidence to include witnesses and perhaps paper trails in the form of receipts. On the other hand they only have their word. They can't remember all of what happened but they disagree that it happened the way you've described. You've got what is known as the smoking gun showing they are completely wrong. All this evidence you've gathered proving them wrong. However something in them will not allow them to believe you are telling the truth. Now, it is affecting the relationship negatively.

Then from a small still voice within you comes

reason. Yes the voice of reason. And this is what it

says, "You have known this person a long time. It's

true, they are not perfect but neither are you. I know

you feel disrespected, but take this time to show that

Love of God. And just forgive this whole situation.

Let it go for righteous sake! Being alone with your

rights does not feel good. A whole relationship

affected negatively, because you are standing on

your rights against their wrongs. There are so many

of us alone today, because we are right and they are

wrong situations. Alone due to, they should know

better and I don't have time to wait for them to

change. What if God took that same position? Where

in the world would human kind be? Wisdom enters

and causes you to measure the price or count the

cost of the relationship. Never mind that they are not

moving from their stance. Never mind that they

should care too about the loss of respect in the

relationship. With the love of God in your heart and the voice of wisdom in your ear, you must respond a better way, by faith hoping for a better outcome. You are not to respond to what you think they should be doing. You must respond according to what God has placed in you. Now you come to know: Sometimes you must give up your right for someone else wrong! Think for a moment: There are relationships that could have been saved. There are people who were doing the best they could to love you but once you saw their flaws you could not handle it, because you have not handled your flaws. One of the biggest flaws of us is not handling others flaws. Not loving each other past the flaws. It is difficult mainly because our flaws are standing deep in the way. When our flaws are handled we are quick to allow and love others in their flawed areas. Go through your life and see the relationships. Perhaps they could not live with your flaws but you lived with theirs.

Give them this book. It will be a truth for those who have ears to hear and eyes to see.

The Only Way To Keep A Secret Between Two Is If One Of You Are Dead

---

Tried and it is true. Even if you are Besties, your secret is not staying with the two of you. Do not fall for the secret handshake or the secret password. We must be sure if our best friend is really our best friend and not someone else best friend too! Because your best friend might have a best friend and their best friend might have a best friend. And so on it goes. So who really is the secret keeper starts with you. Keep your mouth shut! Take it to the Lord in prayer and leave it there. Some people talk so much they forget who they told the secret. Oh, but "It" is a secret! If "it's" a secret, keep it. Prove "it!" If I know and you know then it is not a secret anymore. Hello! When your BFF[6] is upset for some reason of convenience or inconvenience, you best believe your secrets are all told. Even Jesus said go and tell no one, however the word spread. "And He gave them orders not to tell anyone; but the more He ordered them, the more widely they continued to proclaim it." (Mark 7:26 New American Standard Bible) In Humankind keeping secrets does not work. The only way is that one of you who know the secret is dead.

There Is More Than One Way To Skin A Cat

If you ever had the best laid plans and had them fall apart in front of you, then when Grandma said, there is more than one way to skin a cat, became your best friend. Too often when heading in one direction we come across situations that cause us to change directions. It is

---

[6] BFF is acronym for 'best friend forever'

not easy seeing your plans *go up in smoke*, or *down the drain*. However your end results may still happen if you know what Grandma said. There is more than one way to skin a cat. Find it and continue your journey. Finding that other way keeps peace and allows for less stress. Don't be stuck. Instead of starting at the head, perhaps start at the tail. Now I must tell you that skinning a real cat is not the real story here. It is only figuratively.

Two Wrongs Don't Make A Right

Marriage is in the eye of the beholder. We know when we are joined to one another. However, when you know something is wrong, do not repeat. Do not revenge. When you don't like what happened to you, don't cause it to happen to someone else. Don't expect someone to get over what you could not forget. Do not hurt someone just because you can. Knowing hurt, helps us determine when we hurt. Wrong is wrong it can never be right. Nevertheless, you can forgive. Your forgiveness

does not make the wrong right. Forgiveness cause you

to move on from the wrong. The wrong was not right and

you with your forgiveness have decided to live and not

die. When you go after someone with the intent of

revenging, you stagnate only yourself. When you are

hurt- "done wrong by someone", call on forgiveness

quickly. The longer you stay in unforgiveness the longer

the wrong rules and that should never be right.

You Can't Argue By Yourself

This statement is powerful. Many of relationships

could be saved if only this rule was followed. Being

quiet. Listening. Hearing. Noticing. Before we open the

mouth. The mouth can remain close and speak volumes.

The heart can open while the mouth is closed. This

prevents your lips being loose causing ships to sink. The

ship is the relationship. Listening instead of preparing

your counter argument shows more wisdom, than speaking big words. If thoughts of what you did right and what they did wrong are going through your mind, you are not listening, you are preparing your counter argument. That process works best in the courtroom, not in the bedroom. Be quick to hear by listening and slow to speak by caring. And that is all I got to say about that!

You Must Ease Your Head Out Of The Lion's Mouth

I thought why my head would be in a lion's mouth. Grandma said, "Some situations can become dangerous and making a lot of noise could cause you to get hurt, but if you keep calm, and do not get angry, you will survive." Realizing when you are in a scary, dangerous, or frantic situation is good, but surviving those situations with little or no harm will require wisdom.

Situation #1

You have a job. You got the job because you needed a job. Now the boss or supervisor is nagging you. He is getting too close to you while giving a piece of his mind. You got the job because you needed a job, should come to your mind. Sharing your piece of mind with him, is not wise. You could be looking for another job tomorrow if you share today. The loss of your job is that lion's mouth slamming down on your head. LOL! On the other hand, you are much wiser these days and you take your thoughts to the Lord in prayer.

Sometimes we go into situations thinking they are ideal for us. Relations, jobs, rollercoasters. Then we realize we could have made a better decision.

Situation #2:

Jumping out of line while waiting for the rollercoaster ride is good, but while you are on the highest point of the ride is not good. That high point represents the lion's head slamming down on your head. Easy does it! Don't jump out. Hold on! Easy does it! Ride the ride until the end. Wait until the conductor allows you to stand and step out safely. Wipe your forehead. You have eased your head out of the lion's mouth.

Appearance and Health

Cleanliness Is Next

To Godliness

I thought this meant I had to bathe more than usual.

But this cleaning had to be done by God our creator. It

had to be done daily. As a child I overheard an adult say

something about children when they came in from play.

One of the adults said, "These children smell like little

puppies". I went to one of the children and discreetly sniffed them without their permission. The odor I presumed was a little puppy's odor. I calmly placed that odor in my memory bank for future use. I also noticed the heavy sweat on the foreheads of the children. I did not want to be called a little puppy. I did not want to "smell like a little puppy". Whenever I went out to play I felt my skin, if I felt moist, in I went to shower. Shower and a new outfit for play. I changed clothing so often I starting making my own clothes. Hand sewing them all. Halter tops, short pants and miniskirts. My Mother had the skills of a seamstress. She could design and sew together outfits that would rival the runway designer. She taught me some techniques and from there I went. I could overhear the children saying, she always changing clothes. It did not bother me because, I would continue this until I knew how to play without risking "smelling like a little puppy". Deodorant came in handy as I matured. As an adult I know this cleaning the outside was only the half of it. My inside needed cleaning too. Thank God for maturity and wisdom becoming my two best friends. "Create in me a clean heart, O God; and renew a right spirit within me". (Psalms. 51:10 English Standard Version) Having a clean heart created by God and a renewed right spirit inside, not so much outside, makes way for closeness to God.

Drink Warm Water

Warm water is the answer. When you have a headache, drink warm water. When your stomach fill strange, drink warm water. When you have a head cold, drink warm water. Warm water will bring what is really happening to the light. Your headache might be from something else and drinking warm water will move to the point of origin. Shake your head if you dare, but don't knock it until you try it. When those who lived through much worst times than you, advice you to do a thing, it would behoove you to try it. Yes, and believing it helps! If your side has a pain in it, drink warm water. If your back hurts. If a sharp pain shoots through you quickly, scaring the mess out of you, guess what, drink warm water.

Easy Baking

No one could separate me from my Grandma. I watched her move about. She taught me how to bake biscuits from scratch. I entered her kitchen and there she stood with the big bowl in front of her. There was flour in the bowl. I asked what she was doing. She simply said, "Making biscuits." My entering and asking questions did not prevent her from mixing when suddenly onto the cookie sheet and into the oven they went. Quick! I scratched my head in astonishment! She looked at me and asked, "What is it"? I could not hide my feelings. I said, "How did you do that so fast"? She smiled then said, it's easy. What ingredients do you use? I wanted to know how to make them too! Grandma began sharing her recipe for homemade biscuits. Once I returned home, you know I made me some biscuits! Yes! They are delicious to this day! I told you Grandmas are "Gifts from God".

Eat Your Vegetables

How many times have you been told eat your vegetables? Yes we can see it on commercials, hear it at school from teachers and TV shows. How many of us really ate our vegetables. But Grandma said eat your vegetables and you ate them. Why? Because she stood right beside you until you finished. Eating vegetables is a way of getting super powers, at least that is how they promoted them. Then one day years later you turn on the TV and you hear, Escherichia coli outbreak on broccoli. LOL! What is a person to do? Steam the heck out of the vegetables, then eat your vegetable.

Everybody Need A
Hug Every Day

Grandma was correct about this too. The longer you go without a hug the rougher you get; the lonelier you become. Have you tried getting a hug every day from someone? Making getting a hug and giving a hug apart of your daily rituals, would fulfill your life greatly. Moreover, someone else too! Touch is very important. Babies prematurely born are required to be touched, held or rubbed each day as often as possible for purposes of stimulating growth. The time took to properly touch is a gift, not to be misused. The hugs are not sexual hugs but the hugs Grandma said would contain genuine care. A hug is an international form of physical intimacy in which two people put their arms around the neck, back, or waist of one another and hold each other closely. If more than two persons are involved, this is informally referred to as a group hug. (Wikipedia, the free encyclopedia)

If we would hug at every greeting instead of simply shaking hands, what a better world. Hug your children. Hug your spouses. Hug your parents. Hug your pets. Hug your friends. Hug the delivery person. Hug the preacher. Hug the principal. Hug the store greeter. Hug your coach. These hugs would teach us how to show affection without expecting something in return. Hug it out people! Hug!

Pull My Finger

Grandma said pull my finger. I thought she felt discomfort somewhere in her body. I also thought she knew the location. In my mind, seeing Grandma put her hand over the main area of the pain and saying pull my finger, meant Grandma had to burp. If it were in her chest, she would put one hand on her chest then say pull my finger. If it were in her head, she would put one hand on her head, then say, pull my finger. This was always funny because, in addition, when I pulled Grandma's finger out came a gust of wind from her mouth. A burp that caused me to laugh. She would make this shocked face and I would just laugh aloud even more! She did it every time. I asked her, Grandma how do you burp so easily, she said you pulled my finger. It never worked for me, which lead me to believe Grandma just wanted to cause me to laugh! We always had the burps for laughs. Pull my finger!

Put The Black Stuff Everywhere You See The White

I'm about to color Grandma's hair. I have a question. This was my first time coloring her hair. I did not want the responsibility of turning Grandma's hair green, when the color she wanted is black. I asked one question. Grandma where exactly do you want me to put the coloring. Grandma said, "Put the black stuff everywhere you see the white". LOL Grandma Okay! I got you! I had to compose myself before I could start the process. Wow! We both laughed out loud! Grandma did not care to show her age through her hair only through her wisdom. Oh yeah and Grandma's hair did not turn green.

What's Done In The Dark

You may get away with it for a while but time will soon catch up. When we hide ourselves, we are eventually found. Found by the truth. The truth must be told. What is done in the dark will soon come to the light. Darkness don't last always daytime comes next. We can pretend to be something we are not, but eventually we must face facts. However we choose to phrase it. Grandma said there was a lady who was pregnant but did not want anyone to know. Why not grandma, I asked. She had enough children and getting older too. She also was ashamed, she was still having more. Wow! The days went by and so did the months. She concealed her pregnancy for 9 months that I know of. Nine Grandma, yes nine. Then one busy crowded day as she shopped, she felt a thump! Then another one. Gush out came a flow of liquid. The lady was standing in the middle of the center isle of the store. She was with a few of her friends. They had no idea what was happening. The woman fell to the floor screaming and out came the baby. Everyone was shocked. How this could be, they asked. A baby! I understand Grandma. What's done in the dark will soon come to the light.

You Happy, You Happy
Because Your Hair So Nappy

When I first heard Grandma say this, I was shocked!
But Grandma's next words made the situation clearer.
Grandma said, "Come here let me comb your hair". She
could get me to laugh every time from then on whenever
I heard her repeat that statement. That was Grandma's
way of saying it's time to comb your hair. Nappy was not
an unkind word when Grandma said it and it should not
be unkind for people who have nappy hair. Nappy hair
simply describes your hair when it has not been combed
or brushed. Nappy hair does not belong to one race of
people. Let you hair go uncombed beyond your normal
wear and the state your hair turns to is called nappy.
Grandma could plait hair in such a way that your hair
would grow beautifully! Sure Grandma knew I was

tender-headed[7] and I did not like other hands in my head. Why? Because when we touch, we touch with something. It could be a bad attitude, or I've had a rough day, touch. Most people say sit down I got to do your hair. Not me, "I'll do it myself", I'd say. Sticking the comb in and grabbing tightly hurts. I can feel each follicle as my hair was being combed. My hair might be nappy to you but head is tender to me. When I combed my daughter's hair, I always called on Jesus. When Grandma saw me laughing she knew, my hair was not combed. You happy, you happy, your hair so nappy! Yes it is, but I'll do it myself.

---

[7] Tender-headed: I do not like others pulling my hair while combing. I preferred a soft touch.

8

Intimate Relations

A Drunk Man Can't Do
Nothing For Me

Having a drink or two is acceptable. Except if the two

drinks will make you drunk. Leave them off. Drunk is out

of control. Control is much needed. Men often want to

take the lead. Leadership is just that leadership. Leading

someone somewhere. Being a drunk leader leads to

other drunks. Men who lead and are drunk can't lead

where I want to go. When I say men, I'm referring to women too! They can't do what I need them to do. Their performance lacks. Being drunk tells of another problem. Go take care of the problem. Because a drunk man can't do nothing for me. It also tells that he is not ready to take care of you. Drunkenness means you are not in your sober mind. Your actions are out of your control. You can't take care of yourself or me. "And take heed to yourselves, lest at any time your hearts be overcharged with surfeiting, and drunkenness, and cares of this life, and [so] that day come upon you unaware". (Luke 21:34, King James Version), Being drunk, you are not sober. Anything you set your mind to do is not of sober mindedness. All your bodily function are off. You are not really who you were created by God to be when you are drunk. Some people use being drunk as an excuse to being mean, or lazy. It takes work and sometimes hard work to relate to others with positivity. Many people become overwhelmed with nervousness from everyday living, and drinking to them calms nerves which for some translates to courage. It is false courage. It really shows your fear very clearly to anyone who has eyes to see. Eyes to see comes from God. Those who have those eyes will know to pray for you in that situation. But please try to be ever present by being sober and not drunk because, a drunk man can't do nothing for me and that goes for women too!

Buying A Man Shoes Is A Sure Way To Send Him Walking Out Of Your Life

Hearing this, I thought can't buy shoes. Whoa! I asked Grandma, does this apply to everybody? The following is what I heard: When in a relationship gift giving has meanings. The gift that is given also has meanings. And giving shoes to the one you are in relationship with is a sure way of sending them walking away from you. One day I took Grandma shopping to one of her favorite locations. Grandma was thrifty. She spotted some shoes she wanted to buy my then boyfriend, and I immediately remembered her statement. I said Grandma, "I can't purchase these," as I pushed them back towards her. She insisted they be purchased and bought them herself. They were nice shoes and he wore them with pride after I told him the story of Grandma purchasing them. Long story short, we've been married 23 years with two of the most wonderful children who are now adults in College, at the writing of this page. Faith is what you believe; I believed Grandma and it became evidence to me. Grandma purchased the shoes and gave the shoes. You may choose not to believe this, but I did. Think: How often have you wondered what happened to cause your relationship you thought was going good to go bad. If only you could remember who bought the shoes!

Giving A Watch As A Gift To Your Partner Runs The Time Out Of Your Relationship

When Grandma said buying a watch during a relationship and giving it as a gift to the one you love, surely will run the time out of your relationship. I quickly thought, that makes sense. I remembered seeing a TV show and later hearing about a person retiring and as a gift a Golden Watch was given. Retirement means you are not required to work. The job is ended. You can leave now. So, sure giving a watch would run the time you spend together out. Some marriages use watches instead of rings. I wonder are they still married. The marriages I know of who gave watches were divorced years ago. A notice of, I'm leaving you was given. If you want to tell a person goodbye do it with a watch. I dare you to try it. On the other hand if the watch stopped working the relationship will continue. LOL!

Giving Is Good,
But Receiving Is A Gift Too

This lesson Grandma taught me while using another person as an example. As stated before Grandma gave tokens out each Sunday she attended Church Services. But, on this particular Sunday it became clear to Grandma that this person did not want what she was sharing. As I approached her, she began to tell me, how this person would only take candy and never the other goodies she'd prepared. And this particular Sunday they walk by hurriedly. Out came those infamous words from her lips. "Giving is good, but to receive is a gift too"! It seemed she was still speaking these words about the before mentioned person but they spoke to my heart! I received that day in a way I was not expecting. I begin listening in a different way, seeing in a different way even giving differently. There will be those who would say they were taught this same lesson but if you are not a receiver in the same bless way that you give you have not learned. I learned to receive that day. Grandma taught me how to give and now she has taught me a better way to receive. No more wondering why they are giving to me. No more, wondering what this will cost me; suspecting others. I applied this lesson to my daily life. With the words, thank you. Receiving causes us to say, thank you! Many do not like saying those two words, thank you, and really be thankful! Yes, receiving is a gift too, helped me with my spiritual walk! I received from God differently! There is an intention in me to receive from God all God Wills for me!

I Dreamed About Fish

This is what Grandma said right before she spoke about someone being pregnant.

Me: Fish Grandma?

Grandma: Yes fish

Me: Why?

Grandma: Someone is pregnant.

Me: Oh, okay!

Grandma: Whenever I dream of fish, someone in the family is pregnant.

If Your Breast Itch

If your breast itch someone who you had sex with is thinking of sex. Are they still with you? Are they with someone else? Neither matters if your breast itch they are thinking of having sex. This could be a telling sign of cheaters if you ever want to utilize it. And it can tell you they have moved on if your breast are itching and the relationship has ended. If you are not with the person simply give them a call if you are interested. If not wash and oil your breast. LOL, Grandma!

If You Have A Baby And The Man Does Not Want To Marry You Try Another One Don't Have Two By Him

Grandma said, "If a man does not marry you after you have given him a baby, try not to have another one by him. I know having babies are a treasure however, when the man who impregnated you, does not want to marry you, he does not see your worth. I know that if you stay after he does not marry you and have another baby by him, then it appears you do not know your worth. Take your baby and love your baby. Move on. There is another man for you to love. Sure, there are different situations to cause a woman and a man not to marry after having a baby.

Situation #1

Money -having it or not having it is an issue. For some men money is already owed to other mothers; or the government, called child support or taxes. The man says to the woman I would marry you but they would come after your money too for child support. Thinking about this. Why would you add to the mix another baby? Another mouth to feed. He did not say he does not care for the baby or its mother, only he cannot support them financially. Since he cannot support them, it stand to reason he cannot support you financially. Perhaps you enjoy working and will support the baby and him. That is your choice. Just be real with yourself.

Situations #2

Social Security-Some men will not get jobs, which will help support, for the same reason. He will say. They will run my Social Security Number and when that happens the back child support will kick in. Okay! Life is not fair. He could be a great person. However, how could he be great if he has not realized his greatness? Unless his greatness is soliciting you the woman to take up the cross, the baby, the job, for him. Watch the trick he plays on the caring woman. Wake up men.

Daughters and sons be advised and raise your sons to be great men and your daughters to be wise women. Great men to the one they find to marry. I'm aware marriage is in the eye of the beholder. If one of the hopes of your relationship is to own a house are any other property, then having your relationship on paper helps. If you both love each other that should be all that matters. However, for government sake, your love should drive you to the court house or clergy personnel, and printed in black and white. When the emergency happens and answers to who belongs to whom are needed, what will yours be? One of the saddest times is at funerals and the other family arrives with just as much clout as the one who has been taking full care of the deceased. Paper work could alleviate this. Life offers many avenues these days. However if you are starting out and have one baby and are not married, don't add an adult that does not own their worth or yours. What Grandma said is not to judge you but to guide you to getting to your true worth.

If You Must Have Sexual Intercourse, Make It with Only One Person

Having sexual intercourse has a high chance of leading to several situations, pregnancy being one. There have been incidents of a woman accusing a man of being the father of the baby, but later, found not true. 50% here 75% there, what does the DNA say? Child support paid in full monthly for 18, years, but no DNA test taken, just trusting the woman. Oh no she didn't, you can hear the voices say. How could she do him that way? Ladies do yourself a favor and have only one man at a time. That does not mean one a night, or one a month. It means one. If you break up with your sexual partner, lay off for at least 3 months before you move on to another sexual partner. I know people say, we have needs. But cool your needs and think, be wise and consider the mess you could be creating. I'm keeping it 100! Okay? This is not just a fix for pregnancy. It also works for STDs (sexual transmitted diseases). I'm just saying. Lay off for health sake too! I'm not passing out shame, only truth. Those who have ears to hear, hear.

Momma's Baby
Daddy's Maybe!

Grandma said there are women who lied to men. The lie told by the women to the man is, "This is your baby." Looking over life and seeing the lives of those involved hurt. The hurts happened mainly because:

- Some of the women clearly knew they were incorrect.

P a g e | 100

- Others lied because they had not a clue.

- Some women lie because they thought the real daddy could not or would not claim the baby as his.

- And money. One man had it and the other one did not.

- Popularity. One man was and the other was not.

- Kindness. One man had it the other did not.

There are several men who have willingly and unwillingly paid child support, especially prior to DNA testing and some afterwards. The woman's word is all they used to determine the father. The surety was only that the mother was the mother. Moreover, even that became questionable in bad situations. The man needs to apply the rules of life just as the women. Don't go about having sexual intercourse hap hazardly. There are instances when the courts were involved, judges required all the named men by the woman impregnated, to pay child support to the woman. Grandma said mommy's baby daddy's maybe.

The Way You Get Them Is
The Way You Must Keep Them

The time period prior before starting a relationship, any relationship, turns out to be a defining period of the relationship. The way you perform to secure a permanent relationship will become your daily task. If you are the provider, you will continually provide for the success of the relationship. If you gave words of encouragement, you will find you are constantly encouraging your mate. If you find your mate does not get up for work without your help, you will be their constant alarm clock. Most mates who require being awaken by their mate are people who will sleep through the sound of an alarm clock and only awake from the way you've gotten them familiar to awakening. Test your relationship with what I've shared, even the past relationships. Make a list. Write it down. Start with the list below. Answer each question honestly. Determine who started what and who does what in regard to your relationship. Truth time not I'm upset and popping off time. Not I'm trying to make myself look good time. Not I'm trying to win or be right time.

- What caused you to be attractive to your mate?
- Is it still there?
- Are you still expected to perform as you did in the beginning of your relationship?
- Are you expecting your mate to perform as they did in the beginning of the relationship?
- If not, what or who has taken your or their place.
- What is the results?

Use the notes lines to write your response.

Notes:

There Will Come A Time When
We Will Say, There Go A Man

Grandma said her Mother said, there will come a time when we will say, there go a man! What do you mean by this Grandma? Grandma said, she asked her Mother the same question and this is what she said: Women will be sitting on the porch talking and watching as folk walk by, and every now and then, they will spot a man. The woman will be in awe because seeing a man will be scarce. What look like a man will not necessary be a man. Perhaps it will be a male. However when you see a man, you will say to yourself, now that is a man. He will be responding like man, not like an animal. He will be responding like a man, not like a woman trying to look like a man, a man. He will respond like a man, not like a male who is actually more a woman. His response to a woman will be as a man should be, and you will know. Now let me clarify: The previous statements are based on what Grandma said her Mother

Said. I know thanks be to the Spirit of God, that God made man in His image. God is neither male nor female. God is not a respecter of persons. Being a man is more than what one is born with between his legs. Much like being a woman is more than what one is born with between her legs. Knowing who you are and being who you are is one of the main indications of manhood and womanhood. As Grandma said, a man shoots-off[8] and a woman-comes[9]. There go a man, means the behavior of a man toward others. How he treats others; him knowing how he prefers to be treated is a sign of a man. Today we experience these differences of manhood. We are all kinds of humans.

- Some inside do not match the outsides
- Some outsides do not match the insides
- Some desires are bi, desiring both male and female sexually and emotionally

[8] Shoots-off: when a man ejaculates
[9] Comes: when a woman's arousal ends in ejaculation

- Some are male born and desire males sexually and emotionally
- Some are female born and desire females sexually and emotionally.
- Some female born desire males sexually and emotionally
- Some male born desire females sexually and emotionally
- Some are men and women and do not act on any sexual desires
- Some men dress like women
- Some women dress like men
- And there are others...

Grandma said this to me it was the 1980's. I received that wisdom and was better prepared for these days. Did the behaviors simply change? I say no way. Humans have always been made this way. The will to fit in was just too strong. Now that will has weakened considerably. Whatever your state it was already set to happen. Grandma said to me, One day we will see a man and it will really stand out, because what look like a man won't necessarily be a man: according to what once was defined as 'a man'. Being able to discern will be highly needed. Looks will be deceiving if you use the old standards of what constitutes the makeup of man and woman. What is a man is in the eye of the beholder. What say you?

I say:

_____

_____

_____

_____

_____

_____

_____

While Dating Have More Than One Friend

I can remember thinking Grandma just came right out and said that. Wow! Later I recalled how real Grandma was. Life will cause you to make decisions that may not make you the popular one. The choices we make don't always lead to happy times. Some of us come out feeling sad and shameful while others who can hide their wrongs better sleek through life looking from the corners of their souls; Wondering if ever the hidden pieces will become known. The dating game. Having more than one. This is not smiled upon for young ladies. However if you are a young man, they say sow your oaks. Well who do you think he is to sow them with? I realize these days' oaks are sown in several ways, with several types of people. Grandma said have more than one friend to date. Don't tie yourself down so fast. But if you must sow your oaks, only sow with one. Sowing oaks refers to sex. Any kind of sex. Any time bodily fluids transfer. Any time penetration of any part occurs. Knowing that sexual feelings are one of the most natural feelings to us, telling people not to have sex does not always work. High levels of Intelligence is not a factor. Humans enjoy and need sexually communication. It is a part of ministry. The Monks and others who have accepted the call not to sexually participate, have fallen in love with a spiritual being and therefore transmit sexually intimacies on other levels. Some even respond in what is illegal-intercourse with the underage. Humans desire intimacy.

Grandma's point is, if you have more than one friend it may prolong the emotional attachments that develop when you are in a monogamous relationship. These words of Grandma contained a twofold purpose. Can you understand the points? Anybody who has ever had any relationship would know the more time you spend with a person or thing, the better the chances of stronger emotional attachment. The thing being machines or gadgets. Doing these times spent, ways to relate better to one another is established. This is a form of intimacy. And yes intimacy is not found in every relationship but every emotional staked relationship has intimacy all over it. Intimacy is the best cause for a successful relationship. The more you really know each other the safer you feel with one another. Of course, when we have our first emotions of in love, we think we can have them for only one. This is true. Because when we feel it again, it(love) will have the memory of the first emotions of love. Having more than one dating partner is wise if you are not ready for commitment. Sexual behavior peeps into the relationship when time is spent one on one. So have friends but choose wisely. The one you choose today just might be a disappointment to you tomorrow. And yes you will carry them with you into your next intimate relationship.

I'm Just Saying

Don't Place Your Hat
Below Head Level

As Grandma walked through the front of the house, I
could hear Grandma say, pick up that hat and put it on the
closet shelf. Then, I overheard her say, "you should never
place your hat below your head level, as she walked into
another room, It's not good". I might not remember this
verbatim, but Grandma said it was not good for your hat to

go below your head level. If you do, it would mean you have low morals and standards. Low thoughts. I suppose that is why closet shelves are high up instead of low near the floor.

Don't Place Your Purse On The Floor

Wondering why you keep running low on cash, notice where you place your purse or wallet. Grandma said if you pace your purse on the floor, your money would get low. The floor is the lowest level in any room. You can go into the tallest building, enter any room, look around that room, find the lowest point, and it will be the floor. Where we put our money gives it directions. Things don't just happen. We cause then to happen. Cause and Effect. Cause being why an experience happens. Effect is an experience that happens because of a cause. There are consequences to our actions! How we care for what God has afforded us, allows others to see how we are thankful

for what God has giving. How we care for what we
worked for, is a good indication of what happens to what
we work for. When you see money on the ground or floor,
don't you immediately want to pick it up? Sure you do. Up
is what you want your Checking and Savings to be. More
than down! Place your cash in order in your wallet, Take
time to evenly lay each piece. Turn the heads of the
Presidents the same way. Keep as less coins as possible
in your wallet or purse. Place the dollar bills in order from
highest to lowest. Place your purse or wallet high not low.
No this is not an obsession. Don't take it too far.
Everything with moderation. Keep peace in your mind. Do
this when you have time or take the time. But do apply
this mind set to your purse or wallet. Do not put your
wallet in a crowded draw; it will crowd out your cash.

Everyone Has A Bottom

This is true in most cases literally but certainly

figuratively. The time I hit bottom may or may not be

when you hit yours. Believe me there is a bottom to hit.

Life has offered situations mostly cause by each of us,

that we find ourselves in. Some good results and some

bad. Often we are embarrassed to admit we have erred

in our decisions. Decisions that allow us to be perceived

as not so wise. Some people continue on that road of

bad unsuccessful decisions, being driven purely by

pride. Fear of appearing even lesser than the person

who has found you wanting. Some decide to stop look

and listen. Turn from their wicked ways and repent. The

timing of either person in any given situation depend.

What cause one person to quit smoking after years of

smoking once they have been warned of health

dangers? What causes a person to continue to smoke

after being warned of health risk? What causes a person not to smoke, ever? Brings us back to those bottoms we all have. What does it take for a person to care beyond themselves? That is the question. To cause a person to not start a habit that those who love them might one day emulate. You may survive but will your child or your grandchild. Your bottom might not be their bottom. And death is not the ultimate end but, a long painful life ending in death might be the bottom. I used smoking as the example, however drinking, gossiping, over eating, unbelief, miss use of any drug, or any behavior that has been noted as some form of health risk, spiritually or physically, is the behavior a person can exhibit prior to hitting bottom.

If Your Left Ear Itch

Then someone in your present or past is speaking badly about you. Normally I ask God who is speaking bad about me. I immediately hear the person's name. Then I   pray for them. I've lived long enough to know when someone speaks badly about me they need a good prayer. I use this as a spiritual outreach tool.

If Your Left Eye Jumps

Whether or not you are ready for visitors they are on the way. If your left eye jumps someone is coming to see you. Once they get there the news will not be good. Bad news is the left eye jumping friend. Bad news bearer. If you think for a moment, the person's name will come to you. When you get to the correct name your eye will stop jumping. Don't be surprised, it might be your best friend or some other unexpected named person. If you do not want the news rebuke it in Jesus name. It's either that or your nerves are going bad.

If Your Left Hand Itch

Never know when you about to pay out money. Need to be reminded bill payment time. Well listen to your left hand. Your left hand itch conveys you will be paying out some cash. Maybe you will give some away. It's okay, at least it also conveys you have it to pay or give.

If Your Right Ear Is Itching

There are several instances for right ear itching.

1. Someone who loves you now is thinking about you.

2. You are speaking and are feeling self-conscience about what you are sharing

3. Your subconscious thinks the person or

    persons you are addressing do not believe

    what you are saying

    a. And you do not blame them, because

        you do not believe what you are saying.

I've witness from public speakers.ie, Preachers, Political

Officials. Test the theory.

If Your Right Eye Jumps

Good news! When your right eye jumps, someone is

speaking well about you. Someone you know is

charming you up. Someone is bringing you good news.

Look forward to hearing from them. Mostly it is someone

you have not heard from recently. Either way you are

receiving good vibes from someone in the universe. You

may be in what is considered a bad situation, then your

right eye jumps. That should tell you that your situation is looking up. Think positive someone else is, and it's all about you.

If Your Right Hand Itch

If you feel your right hand itching, scratch. Grandma said, that means money is coming. Money will come to you. You could be cleaning out an old purse, and you will find some money. Perhaps you are walking in a store, then your hand itch, you look down, and see money in some sort of form. It's yours, pick it up. The denomination does not matter. Pick the money up. Be faithful over a few things and God will make you ruler over many. This works if you truly have a right hand that itches and you truly believe.

It Does Not Matter
A Hil-A-Being

The following statement contains slang. Grandma said it does not matter *a hil-a being* what they say. Translation: It does not matter high or low here or there, heaven or hell, or who said it. This phrase is use to show there is no difference in any of us. We are the same. Your position does not matter. A person's lot in life is not important. People are people. And what that person said is not important as they claim it to be. It does not matter to you. It is not a factor over you circumstances. It does not matter *a hil-a-being.* Best use: when someone throws insults. Simply say to yourself, It does not matter a hil-a-being!

10

Sowing & Reaping

If It Don't Get You In The Washing It Will Get You In The Rinsing

---

Being disobedient is what this is about. Most

times bad things happen, we wonder why. The main

reason we wonder why is because we quickly forget

the bad things we do. Often we do not acknowledge

our wrong doings at the time we are performing

them. Too much time passes without recognizing our

wrongs; not having eyes to see and ears to hear. Sometimes we use not remembering as an excuse. However, when the bad that we do immediately returns to us we have a better chance of recalling the bad we've committed. Time passes but the bad we do does not. It will show up one way or the other in our lives. It will reveal to us the actions we prefer to forget or never be reminded of. We are better off confessing our faults, at least to ourselves if not to those we've wronged. There is no reason standing around looking for answers when the solution is in us. Remember we are set to meet our wrongs and rights again face to face. If it don't get you in the washing it will get you in the rinse.

Pointing Your Finger Means You Have Three Fingers Pointed Back At You

Grandma said, pointing your finger means you have three fingers pointed back at you! She said try it! I pointed my finger (index finger) and surely there were three fingers pointing back at me. Go ahead you try it. If you don't try it, it's because you already know, don't you. Finger pointing is done usually when someone else contends that another is wrong or has caused the situation: usually not a happy time. Lesson: When I think someone else is wrong; I am three times as wrong. Finger pointed helps you not focus on yourself. The illusion of I'm right and you are wrong is in full effect. The reality stands opposite of that illusion. The wrong you see, is in you. Stop looking so hard at the other person and tune into your reality. How do you know when you are finger pointing? Who is the object of your emotional state of mind? Examine your happiness, your anger, your joy, your health condition, or whatever your part in what cause you to finger point as you sit still; be quiet. Finger pointing is a good way of finding out who is wrong. I give you three guesses!

She Could Be Someone's Mother Or Daughter, Keep That In Mind

There was this woman who enjoyed a drink so much she would get drunk and fall out! One night she did just that. She fell out while drinking with some fellows as they sat behind a billboard sign. They proceeded having sex with her. The lady did not awaken. This went on long enough for each to have his turn. The word spread about the woman behind the billboard sign, being ready, able, and a good lay. One at a time the males went and came from behind the sign; zipping up their pants, urging the next feller of his turn. The woman's skirt was pulled up over her head. Her face concealed; her identity unknown. The men continued. One of the men, stood up while behind the sign so happy and satisfied. He shouted for all who could hear," I don't know who she is but she got some good stuff." He then said, "I want to know who this is", and pulled her skirt from her face revealing his own mother as the woman. He became nauseous, as he ran from the location. The saying is nobody has seen him since! Moral of this story, you should be able to guess. Do unto others as you would have them do to you. Do unto to others as if it is your Mother it is being done to. That woman could have been someone's mother and she was, someone's daughter and she was. We are loved by someone. We are special to someone. Someone cares for that person who was just violated. Look away, run away, or just stay away from getting yours without considering others.

Stomach Wet Is
A Sign Of Laziness

This disturbed me. The subject it refers to is washing dishes. Leaning against the sink, makes for wet clothing, when the water splashes. You know standing in one place, after a while, your feet hurt. You may lean against the sink to brace yourself. Then with a swish of the water out comes a splash. Landing on your clothing. I know Grandma was teaching me a lesson or two with that statement.

1. Don't fill the sink up with too much water

2. Don't lean against the sink

3. Don't take too long to wash the dishes

4. Don't wait until you are tired before you wash the dishes

5. Wear an apron

Grandma was teaching me to stand strong on my feet. Leaning shows you are not taking what you are doing seriously. No preparation. Timing yourself. Knowing how to stand strong, makes for you being pushed over difficult. Wet clothes is a sign of how much or little you cared for your duties. With any water container there is a possibility of a splash. Think beforehand how to prevent the splash from ending up on your attire. It could be the bathroom sink. It could be the public restroom. Grandma used an apron and kept a towel for drying her hands nearby. I used aprons and if by chance I wet my stomach, I begin fanning my clothes. But if that did not hide the splash, I'd change quickly. It's funny but with wet clothing you can catch a cold too! Thanks Grandma.

There's A Good Laugh
And A Bad Laugh

We hear laughing is good for the soul. Yes it is. However, there's a good laugh and a bad laugh. How can a Laugh be bad? Some might ask. Some might even disagree by saying laughing could never be bad. Let's look at laughing.

- Laughing at jokes
- Laughing at yourself
- Being laughed at
- Laughing to keep from crying, etc.

Have your pick. Laughing becomes bad when use to bash another's spirit. You might say, I'm just having fun. But the one who is being laughed at without permission is not having fun.

Without permission is:

- Someone slips and fall. Laughter erupts. Do you know if the person has injured themselves? Check to see if they are physically okay, then emotionally, before you find their fall funny.
- Someone is at a public gathering and begin to tell a story that involves someone who has not given me permission to tell their part. Not funny without permission buddy!

Permissive Laughter:

- Someone is on stage and telling what happened about their life during comedy night
- Somebody is being roasted at a celebration dinner by family and friends
- Someone might say let me tell you something then proceed to tell a story strictly about themselves

Bad laughing. You might say I was just joking. If you have to say you are joking, then you just had a bad laugh. And please don't say you were just playing. You play with toys not with people's emotions. Some people have a nervous laugh. Some people laugh to be agreeable. When you asked what is funny, they shrug their shoulder. These are cultural behaviors we can change immediately in the world to show true Godly Love. Start with your immediate family. If you have been exhibiting bad laughter STOP! No gradual slowing down, STOP! These lessons in laughing need to be implemented at early childhood. But adulthood is a good time if now is what you have. We could change the culture of bullying. We all say bulling is bad. It causes long term effects. We say we have survived the being laughed at period while growing through our most awkward years. But let's be fully honest. We need to want more than to survive. We need to overcome this behavior. Let's give our children permission to be kind. To tend to one another's emotional state. Let's give ourselves permission to be kind. Let's build the smiles into laughter. If we see or hear something that appears to be funny, take time, look at what or who caused the action. Are they laughing? Was there a smile first? The before mentioned statements are several indicators we must use with maturity. As mature people we have the responsibility to change the culture that we know causes hurt. Let us really be better. Let us laugh like we know it is telling a lot about us, because it is. Smile and the world smiles with you. Laughing can mean you are hiding hurt. Let's look closer to the laughs like we look closer to the tears, for the true origins.

11

Skin Perspective

Black And Die

Often we take everyday life task as necessary. But many of them are not. Grandma said to the person who told her, you must complete this, it must be done, "No", she said, "all I got to do is die". When Grandma said, all I got to do is die. You know I had to ask. What do you mean Grandma? Grandma said, I'm already Black, now all I got to do is die. This is about dying and what must be. When we die we naturally begin to darken. The color of our skin does not matter. From the lightest to the darkest, we all become darker than we were while we were alive. Grandma said we all must die at the appointed time. She knew some are lighter while others are darker. Grandma wanted me to know that she considered herself the darker. She said Black. She is already Black now all she has on her schedule, is that she must die. LOL that's Grandma. This is for all who think they have a lot to do before they die.

Blacker Than A V8 Ford

Recalling when I heard Blacker than a V8 Ford took me to being pregnant with my first born. My body went through several changes. The one of interest, is I got darker in certain areas of my body. The obvious area is my neck. On a particular day of shopping with Grandma she took one look, and out came, your neck is darker than a V8 Ford! As she laughed at what she obviously considered a funny statement, I looked at her. Here's Grandma laughing because she has cracked a joke. I started laughing too! I researched V8 Fords to see how black they are. Yes they are Black and my neck and ankles where too! To some this might offend, but to me it did not. I'm proud of being black. I was born that way! Now all I got to do is die!

I Been Drinking Buttermilk

Grandma said the young woman said, "I've been drinking butter milk." Why did she say this Grandma? The baby came out... Well let me start from the beginning she said. The talk was that this woman cheated on her husband. Cheated with the white man down the road. The woman denied all accusations. When the baby was born, the baby was quite light almost white. When asked why the baby's color was quite light almost white, she simply said, "I been drinking butter milk." Buttermilk anyone?

If You Are Black You Got To Get Back

During periods of segregation blacks were forced to enter through the back of every building they could enter. Blacks were forced to the back of the line. Blacks were force to the back of the bus. Blacks were forced to eat last. And people wonder why we have what is call CPT (color people time). Black people time was not their own. For generations Blacks moved slower. If a black moved fast it had better be on the authority of the white. Paying at the front of the bus, then, exit, only to re-enter through the side door to sit or stand at the back. All because you are black. Blacks could not try on shoes before they purchased the shoes. Their feet were measure on a piece of paper. Whites did not want you in front of them unless it was wartime. Blacks could fly and

march at the front. And so they did. However as soon as

the wars were over, being black, when they returned

home, they had to get back. Blacks would pay the same

price for racist service. But change was a coming.

Blacks are a chosen and determined race of people. The

blacks who did not flee to more welcoming lands, stood

their ground, with prayer, and violence at times. Blacks

caused change to come to the United Stated of America

and the world. The blacks who did not flee knew

something. They knew they deserved better. And they

did what was necessary to get to that better. They did

not run to another country just because they were afraid

of losing their lives. Many lost their lives. And yes many

were afraid. Not sleeping at night. Many took turns

staying up watching. As I stated before some used

violence. You know there is only so many hard knocks a

person will and can take before there is a concussion.

And you know research has shown that concussions can

cause you to behave a bit out of sorts. Being black and being demanded to get back is a hard knock. And that's all I'm going to say about that!

Is Grandma Black Or White

This question was asked about what would seem obvious, however one could never really know. God created us and we come in many shades of color. During slavery and afterwards, the "white man" would take advantage of the slaves who were black- a darker skinned. Raping both the black male and female is one way the white man took advantage. Both victims were left carrying the painful shame. The woman often left carrying the shame of that rape for all to see, in the form of pregnancy. Consequently, the skin color of some born to the rapped woman with darker skin, became lighter and lighter. The Black mother would birth a baby that often passed as "white". As those children grew into adulthood, and begot children, the skin colors continues to lighten for some and darken for others. Children being inquisitive would ask this question. Grandmas answered the question as best they could. Being that most Grandmas are wise souls. Some Grandmas said, "Grandma is Black baby." On the other hand, some Grandmas said, "That's not your Grandma baby, that's a "white lady". These answers could make or break a life. Telling a black-Slave child her Grandma is White would cause death. Most times when the news got out that Grandma was Black instead of White. Slave owners would sale the lighter skinned Slave. The status of the person stood on the answers-slave or master. Black or White. Some of those behaviors have changed. Today many are still passing either as Black or White. But one thing for sure the Grandmas are still Grandmas.

The Blacker The Berry The Sweeter The Juice

Grandma said the blacker the berry the sweeter the juice! Grandma would say this with a smile. Grandma said the berries get darker and become sweeter! At the sweetest point they are very dark. I took this to thought. My family is a linage of the name Berry. I thought Grandma was being clever. Grandma knew the black man was a beautiful man. I thought she was telling me the blacker the man the better the man. LOL! I could believe this until I knew better. The best man is the man made for you. However the blacker the berry the sweeter the juice still hold steady! Try it! Taste a light berry then taste a darker (black) berry. Taste the berries prior to them turning blacker. Testing, testing, 1, 2, 3. On the other hand there is nothing wrong with knowing the Blacker man is the better man. Black Pride!

12

Testimony

Every Frog Croaks About
His Own Pond

Talking about what you do is considered bragging in

some circles. However when you do what you do, you are

the first to know. Better you tell your tell than another.

Some say it's tooting your own horn! Then I say toot toot!

Many times the story has missing parts when others tell

your story. Therefore, it makes for a better chance of

success story telling when it is told by the main character. Where you are in life should be the best place, why, because you are there. Knowing this will cause for a healthier life. Your home, the school you attended, the car you drive and even your family, are ponds to croak about. Whatever God affords you in life be happy and testify to that goodness!

I'm So Glad I'm Here In Jesus Name!

Grandma's testimony each Wednesday night would start while she sat on the church bench. She'd start with double clapping sound coming from her hands, she would sing,

> Yes I'm ---so- glad--- I'm -here, [Repeat 1X]
> Yes I'm--- so glad-- I'm- here in Jesus name [Repeat 1X]

As the song ended Grandma would slowly stand and begin to speak about the time The Spirit of God came to her in the form of a voice, and gave her much comfort.

She called it the time when God changed my life, a testimony. The testimony when God changed her old life over to the beginning of her new life. With what I know today from Grandma and living, it would be nice if we all could recall when and how God changed us over from the old way of living to a better, newer way. How the old things passed away. How you looked at your hands and they looked new and how you looked at your feet and they did too. I recall sitting listening to Grandma, and looking around at the others look at her. Their faces told stories. I could hear one or two mumble, "why is she telling that story again". Another said, "She should be a shame". Moreover, when Grandma would cry, there were those who asked Grandma, if she was in pain. However, Grandma was on her journey. A journey set by God. Grandma had been delivered from people enough to know God's approval was more valuable than humankind's. Taking time to think if God has changed us or have there been any change at all is an important step in our spiritual life. There is a change, most get confused about. The change happens because you have aged. Getting older and not being able to do what you once did, does not constitute a Godly change. With that kind of change, we will still have the desires, but perhaps do not have the means or the energy to do what we desire. Being young in body and trying to do right or be a good person is not the change of Godliness. God is not interested in our goodness, or who is right; that's only the way of attempting to please mankind. But once God has changed you, the thoughts of returning to your formal self are gone. The desires go too! Oh you will remember your past desires, but they will no longer entice you! It has been shown that God has a Hand. The Hand of God will touch, and change will happen. What God touches, is never the same. "Then the Lord put out his hand and touched my mouth. And the Lord said to me, "Behold, I have put my words in your mouth". (Jeremiah 1:9 English Standard Version) The will to do as we once did, is gone. Being touched by another human is not the change; even if you feel you have changed. This change is between us as individuals, and God. The Bible teaches about the Holy Spirit, which is the Spirit of God, coming to guide us into the real way of Life! When humans touch one another we can go in and out the same way. But when God touch us we go in one way, and leave another; we are thankful for this change and we give God all the glory! You know the change came from the Hand of God. You know without a doubt you are set to living a different way. Better outlook of the days are happening not only to you but also to those who you love! Amen! Hallelujah! Be born again today! Believe and know that God has you safely in Hand! God has made a way for us to walk closer in the Spirit! If you are ready, pray this prayer:

Lord Jesus, I am sorry for my sins, I renounce Satan and all his works, and I give you my life. I forgive all those who have offended me. I now receive and accept you as my personal Lord and my personal Savior, and as I just prayed, by faith, I ask You God to fill me with Your Holy Spirit. Make me believe without a shadow of doubt[10]. In Jesus name Amen.

    1. Have you changed? Yes___ or No___

    2. When did your change begin? (The situation)

_____

_____

_____

_____

_____

_____

_____

_____

---

[10] Shadow of doubt: emphasizing there is no doubt at all that it is true

_____

_____

_____

_____

_____

_____

_____

_____

_____

3. Have you shared your change? (Testify)

How God changed me: (This is a change you can't keep quiet about. It is a strong sensation from within your heart's soul. When others try to silence you with shame, you still share your change, because it is too powerful. The work God has done in you, not just for you, but in you is too strong to keep!

_____

_____

_____

_____

_____

_____

_____

_____

_____

_____

Poor Frog That Does Not Croak About Their Own Pond

Speaking of telling your own story, the opposite occurs when you do not tell your story. Advertisement is a productive way of getting information to others. Telling what you can do is like a resume. It performs for your benefit or against you. I say it's better to know than not. Don't be miss guided and think you are bragging or boasting. When your intention is good they will make good, no matter how it appears. But be clear that your intentions are good. Telling your story is best. Speaking your truth is necessary. Ponds are where frogs live. To live there ponds must possess some form of comfort to frogs. Our places of living should possess the same characteristics. If your place of living is not comforting, then are you really living? The Living should be such that you can't help but share what happens there. It is a tell-tell on us, that we enjoy reality Television. Looking into the lives of others. Seeing somewhat where they live and how they live. While the frog croaks loudly from the pond, we share on FB[11] about our life, which include where we live. It is good to share your story.

---

[11] FB is an acronym for the online social network, Facebook

Sister You Don't Love Yourself

Sister you don't love yourself! This is what Grandma heard the small still voice say. She was feeling sad. She thought, I'm all alone, I'm, all alone, I'm all alone, nobody cares for me, and nobody loves me. As she began to sob, deep in her sadness, a comforting voice came to her and spiritually tapped her on the shoulder. The state of mind Grandma was in caused me to consider, "The righteous cry, and the LORD hears And delivers them out of all their troubles. The LORD is near to the brokenhearted and saves those who are crushed in spirit. Many are the afflictions of the righteous, But the LORD delivers him out of them all...." (Psalms 34:17-19 The New International Version) Meanwhile Grandma said she heard, Sister, you don't love yourself." I realized this was a part of Grandma's Testimony. God was changing her from her old way of thinking to a closer walk toward God's way of thinking. There is a time in everyone's life; we face all the hurts of our life. These times are purposed for change. Surrendering your life over to God happens when we have tried other avenues of life we were able to try to answer our needs, and we now realize those ways cause more harm than good. Some people go through hell on earth, to include, painful breakups, deaths, loss of jobs, loss of respect, and waking up in their own vomit. Fake love of self will lead you to those places. However, when true, love of self happens, goodness is present. The longer you fool yourself into thinking the hurt is supposed to keep happening, the longer you will stay in the lack of true love. Emotionally, this is what causes depression. Missed placed self-love. Drinking until you are drunk or unconscious is not self-love. Not getting proper exercise is not self-love. Not eating a healthy diet is not self-love. When we do not love ourselves we cannot judge Love; either the receiving or the giving of it. "Do not get drunk on wine, which leads to debauchery. Instead, be filled with the Spirit". (Ephesians 5:18 New International Version) As the voice gave Grandma Comfort, she was able to concentrate her sights on God. When we focus on God, God will keep us in perfect peace! Too many of us confuse repetitiveness of attending "Church" as being focused on God. God does not give out perfect attendance certificates man does. Too many of us confuse Tithing and Offering as the best return for goods and services. But God is not concern with our Taxes or their Returns; man is. Trying to please God by pleasing man will only lead us to holding our faces. Man cannot be pleased. You can ask the Children of Israel; who cried hundreds of years to be delivered from their oppressors, only to complain their way back into an oppressed state for 40, years. God could not please them. Nor could Moses, God's Prophet. We become depressed drunks, or druggies. To God, His creation seeking Him faithfully is the key. When we have done all we can and are holding our face, we cry out from a place only God can hear us from. A place only God can bring us from too! Once we have visited that place, I said really visited, we do not want to go again. Some of us think we have been there over and over again, but no. You have went somewhere, but it was not that place of holding your face and crying that only God can bring you from. It might have felt horrible where you went. But if you returned, without change, it was not that place I'm referring. Grandma went there. I've been there. My question to you is have you been there? Evidence of being there:

- Only God can bring you from there
- You never return there
- You remember being there
- Your life is never the same.
- Your view point of others is better, more understanding.
- Your view point of love is unconditional
- Your faith in God is unshakable

- When bad situations present themselves to you, your response is to receive God's purpose from it.
- The places you used to go you don't need or want to go there.
- The people you call friends change.
- The things you did that cause you harm, you don't do any more.

The question is have you been there. The answer is your truth. Change is change. Sometimes we have BIG obvious changes and sometimes we have small centimeter changes. Document your change on the lines provided. If there has not been a change leave the lines blank until your change comes. The time I went there and came back changed

was..._____

_____

_____

_____

13

That Mouth

A Lie Don't Care Who Tell It

Hearing this from Grandma, I believed we all lie. We open our mouths and outcome the words. When asked we have choices; whether to tell our truth or someone else's. The truth rarely escapes our lips. Lying comes too easy to some. At an early age a lie is simpler but as we become adults, lying is difficult. Some lie just to hear the response. Some lie because they were asked a question. Some lie every time their lips are moving. Some wake up lying and some go to sleep lying. The days are long with lies. The night are not too short of lies either! Politicians lie. Teachers lie. Preachers lie. Prophets lie. Apostles, lie. Evangelist lie. Pastors lie. Friends lie to friends. Parents lie to children. Spouses lie to each other. Children lie to parents. The governments lie to taxpayers. Tax payers lie to the government. Employees lie to employers and vice versa. Doctors lie to patients. Patients lie to Doctors. All humankind lies. I had to believe especially when I found these words in the Bible. "God forbid: yea, let God be true, but every man a liar, as it is written, that thou mightest be justified in thy sayings, and mightest overcome when thou art judged" (Romans 3:4 King James Version),

   We lie because the story we tell is according to our perspective. Ask another about the same situation and they will tell the same, a lie, only according to their perspective. The best of us lie and sometimes we blame it all on miss information. We lie by omission or commission.

An omission is a 'failure to act'. When asked to tell the whole truth, but we tell half the truth, we lie through omission. If you lie and you do not know you are lying, it still is a lie. Putting our hand on a stack of Bibles does not make what we are swearing be the truth. Commission is when we know we are about to lie and we follow through with the lie. Yes I know I lied. Yes I needed to lie. As Grandma said, a lie don't care who tells it. I added it (the lie) just want to be told.

If You Lie You Will Steal
If You Steal, You Will Kill

A liar is bad enough. Now a thief too! Whoa! Killing! Because, you will need to cover up what you did, no one wants to be caught! I recall thinking, But Grandma, I have told lies and did not kill anyone. Then a small still voice entered my ears, saying, but you did. Telling a lie steals the chance of truth being heard, and kills the life of a true relationship. The person I lied to only knows my lie. My truth is yet to be told. So really what relating are we doing? It is not a good-ship, because it is not going anywhere good when based on a lie. Testing this method: Think of a lie you told. Come on, you know you have told lies. Okay, you got it. Oh my, you've told so many you're having a difficult time choosing. LOL! Okay! Let's slow down a bit. Wait for it! Wait for it! Now ease into it. Do you have the lie you want to use? Okay, you can't remember one lie. That's a lie LOL! Then think of a lie someone said to you. Place that lie in this context. Did the relationship go anywhere? Are you still there? That relationship is dead. Even if you are still there, you are not there the same way. I rest my case. This was fun! Grandma said it, you lie, you will steal, and if you steal you will kill.

We Can Make Our Mouth
Say Anything

The thought came, the words begin to form and out they go. Out of the mouth flows truth or lies, future happenings or the present situations, life or death. I will be good to you. I will never lie. You can depend on me. A man's word is his bond. Sticks and stones may break my bones, but words will never hurt. One soon realizes words do hurt as well as destroy. Words give life and words take life. The mouth is an avenue used to drive someone to or from. Decide what you want and confess it. The mouth can say what the mind thinks. The mouth can form words that the body can and cannot do. Saying the first words that come to mind is not always the wise choice. Being the quickest to throw shade[12] is not always the way to draw friends. Using your mouth

---

[12] Throw Shade: Insulting someone; revealing a truth the subject of the truth did not want told; does not look favorable on the subject of insult

as a weapon only hurts you. Remember we reap what we sow. If you are reaping it some kind of a way you sowed it. If you would think of your mouth as the avenue it is, you would care what comes out of it. Driving is a serious deed. Running over others with your words is not kind or safe. Just because you've decided that this person deserved the words you issued them, does not make it a Godly move. Some of us are driving without a license. Making illegal turns and running people off the road. The driving metaphor is working for this Grandma said topic. LOL! We can make our mouth say anything. We have this freedom of speech amendment in The United Stated Constitution. This amendment gives citizens of the United States of America the right to speak their minds as long as speaking their minds does not cause bodily harm or proven offense to those around them. I put that amendment as plain as I could, without misleading you. When the crowd shouts let him go police! The police hear their shouts, but will not simply let him go. Our mouths can demand, even request politely, but to no avail. Confession without profession is to no avail. What we say works best when what we say match what we do. But until then, our confession until it comes to reality is what most will do. Making our mouths say anything until something happens.

14

The Funeral

Bye John

When Grandma said, there was a lady who had a
husband name John. One day John died. The lady was
heartbroken. She cried and cried! At the funeral when
the undertakers began to close the casket, the lady
jumped up and threw herself against the casket, holding
the casket open. The undertakers allowed her to
continue until she calmed herself and returned to her

seat. As they began to close the casket again, the lady jumped up again. Sobbing uncontrollably! The undertakers simply stood by and allowed her the time she needed to calm down again. Once reseated the undertakers started closing the casket, immediately the lady jumped up for the third time, and started toward the casket, but this time the undertaker leaned over to her and whispered into her ear, "If we have to open this casket up again it will be $400.00". The lady quickly responded, "Bye John!" LOL! Grandma and I laughed out loud! Grandma said this long before I met and married my husband John. No pun intended!

Just Put Me In A Wooden Box

Grandma said "just put me in a wooden box". I asked her why you want to be put in a wooden box. Grandma said, "Do not put all that money in the ground." Grandma knew the mortuaries are out to make money.

She also understood it is a business, burying people.

There are regulations to follow when burying. The prices

are constantly going up. The wooden box is the box that

the government use when the family confirms the Life

Insurance money will not be used to bury the deceased

or that there is no money for the burial. The wooden box

with the deceased body is carried out to a six feet deep

hole, lowered into the ground by two ropes and two men,

immediately after a prayer. No money exchanged. These

burials are great especially if you are low on funds. The

next level of burial is a wooden box covered with a thin

white floral textured cloth. It feel like velvet. From this

box the prices continue to increase. Grandma would say

take my money and pay the bills, and put me in a

wooden box. Don't make such a fuss over that body. I

took a while to grasp this way of thinking. The longer I

live the clearer I hear Grandma's voice. Many are

preferring cremation over burial. Placing the ashes in a

container. I know if family and friends are going to visit

the grave then yes, do the grave burial, but if your people are not grave visitors, do not buy a grave for them to visit. Cremation all the way. And if you have grave visitors, consider using the wooden box.

You Can't Take It With You

What all we accumulate we can't take with us. Use them while you can. Do well with what you have. Because you can't take it with you. Give to those you wish to give. See them smile at your giving to them. Storing up treasures to share when you are no longer living on earth, is not advised. Saving the best for last or holding on to things not wanting to share. Grandma said, "you can't take it with you". I have heard of people trying to prove this statement wrong. Being buried with their cars. Being buried with their jewelry. As far as they took it, was when their items were placed in the casket by someone else. Therefore, they did not take it with them.

If you dig them up, there you will find their things; if they had honest Undertakers and Cemetery workers. A bit to chew on. Don't wait to satisfy someone. Don't put off tomorrow what you can do today. Your thoughts are just that, yours; until you share. Your plans are just that, your plans; until you share. Your gifts are just that, yours, until you share. Give what you have to give while you are the original giver. Your Will, should be to have given already.

You Live Your Funeral

This is when you hear people stand at the Home Going services and recite your life. The memories you shared with others is publicly announced at your funeral. Grandma wanted me to know the people you touch will talk about it at your funeral and it is nothing you can do about it. Mine who you associate with. The person you are while alive, might not be the person you want others to talk about at your funeral, but they will. All the memories will come flooding back, just the way "they say" it happened. "They say", "she say", will rule on that day. It is good to write your Autobiography before you leave this world. What others will say about you at your funeral is what they are saying about you behind your back. The good things and the bad things. Your conversations are some of the best funeral talks. So I thought, try to be a better person or out live all my friends and family. LOL! Really! I know my family and friends will have good news to share with my children at my funeral. I am living each day as best I can to be a better person than I was the day before. I am trying to live my funeral, are you!

15

Truth Be Told

Crying Is Good For You

Suffering with sinus is a commonality between Grandma and me. They ranged from headaches to stuffiness of the nose. Often I would hurt. I develop a method of not crying. Some of the development came from other situations. The bottom line, I would not cry, I refuse to cry. Never would you see my tears. Grandma would cry quickly. Sometimes I thought too quickly. One

day the sinus pain came heavy upon me, and I landed at

Grandma's Bedside. Grandma my head will not stop

hurting. She asked, had I prayed. Yes, Grandma, I've

prayed. Grandma's next statements included her asking

me do I cry. I immediately responded with a no.

Grandma asked, why. I told her I just don't cry. Really

Grandma, I said, it is difficult for me to cry. I don't know

how to cry any more. Grandma moved to the edge of

her bed, took me by the hands and spoke these word to

me. "Crying is good for you." Strange words to me,

almost foreign. Grandma preceded to teach me how to

cry. Teaching was one of Grandmas Ministries. She said

try Sonya. I asked how. She began to cry for me. I saw

her passion and tears. I started trying really hard to cry.

Oh God help me cry. The pain from the sinus headache

hit me one quick time, the tears began to flow. My

nostrils opened. I could breathe, the headache

alleviated. Yes! Yes! Thank You Lord, thank you

Grandma! Then Grandma said now do not cry too much or it will defeat the purpose. Everything in moderation. A little goes a long way. I was happy and relieved. Grandma said, "Crying is good for you". "It helps release stuff". Sometimes you just don't know how much is on you. Crying with fix it. Cry and let it all out. Don't be shame. Before I had my first child, God visited me. The Holy Spirit fell on me while I was in the fetal position. Scared, frustrated, alone and in the dark. I asked my husband not to interfere. This was between God and me. I began to cry out to God! Please come to me God! The tears came from everywhere. I know God used my tears to wash away a lot of what kept me bound. When it was over, I dried the tears, got up and left that darkness behind. I've walked in the light ever since. Crying is good, it helps release stuff!

Every Generation Gets
Weaker And Wiser

Every generation gets weaker and wiser statement stayed with me since I heard it from Grandma. I heard her say this during my teenage years. I remember asking Grandma how she knew every generation will get weaker and wiser. She said, her mother told her. Grandma also said she thought it came from the Bible. When I started studying the Bible I went in search of this very statement. I could not find it. I went to Grandma as I often did with the question of, Grandma did you say the statement every generation gets weaker and wiser is in the Bible. Grandma replied," it's in the Bible". Grandma I did not find it in the Bible. I wanting her to take me to the chapter and verse; guide me there. But no Grandma said, "Hmmm, you didn't find it, well okay. I do not know why you did not find it, it's true and it is in the Bible". Grandma never argued. As I continued studying the Bible, I came to know this statement. The statement is in the Bible. It is not verbatim. The generations learn. The world changes. We gain and lose. We know something clearly one day and the same subject confounds us the next. Knowing is the sum of not knowing. Being wise and weak at the same time. Jesus was wise and weak at the same time. Jesus allowed himself to be weak enough to be jailed and hung but wise enough to obey the perfect Will of God. The generations are getting wiser. We know more history, because there is more history to know. Wisdom according to Oxford Dictionary, is the quality of having experience, knowledge, and good judgment; the quality of being wise. Our weakness shows gravely through our destruction. Here we are knowing more than we ever have yet are too weak to change without the threat of pain. Some people rather suffer than change. We know we did not create the earth or the heavens. Some people search for the creator and believe nothing because they found nothing they could believe. Their beliefs are based on the weaker parts of us.

That is our knowledge. What we know is but a drop to the floods the creator has before us. From generation to generation we search for answers hidden as if they are hidden from us. It would be well to know that God is in control. We search for answers that are intentionally hid for us. When we are not living by faith those hidden things are lost to us. Faith brings them to our eyes and ears. We refuse wisdom and take up with lack. The lack of knowledge causes us to parish. When we refuse to do better, when we know better we prove we are not wise. Why do we anger at the words stating change must come? For change to come someone would need to acknowledge. And often we stand on the side of prove it to me then I will believe. Like Thomas in the Bible wanting to place our fingers into the wounds of the creator. Holding our belief as a hostage. Ransoming our faith to the highest convincer. Yes Grandma it is written, every generation will get weaker and wiser.

When the spies sent to spy the land came back with a scary report the elders refused to enter the land the Lord gave for them to take. Their eyes sold them on another reality based on the knowledge past gained. The Lord wanted them to move toward faith to gain wisdom and strength; knowing who had brought them safely out of bondage. But the generations of elders could not change. God commanded the weaker ones to move forward and gain the knowledge God had for them. 40 years would stand for the 40 days the spies spied the land prior to returning to give their report. The ones who the elders deemed weak would soon be the wiser. The young ones who were thought to be as prey. God used what appeared as their weaker parts to gain wisdom; their age. Wisdom gained brings sorrow and more knowledge brings grief! This could cause your appearance to appear weak. This weakness is seen through the eyes of man. God does not see it as weakness, but opportunity. Jesus seemed weak to his followers and his persecutors. Jesus' reality is as he saw it, obedience. Jesus knew when we are weak God is our strength. Being seen weak by humankind is a sign of strength. God's strength stand while we may fall. Our enemies never actually see us fall. When by faith we believe God is our strength. Who can stand against us? Yes, we will be weaker and wiser. We will lean on the everlasting arms. We will no longer lean to our own understanding. We will wait on the Lord. Humankind will see us as weak but we will know we are becoming wise. Those of us leaning on the Word of God will gain. There is a bit of secrecy to this weaker and wiser subject. I love it! It's like being hidden in plain sight. Those who do not believe will not be able to enter "But your little ones, which ye said should be a prey, them will I bring in, and they shall know the land which ye have despised" (Numbers 14:31 King James Version)

Everyone Does Not Graduate From High School.

It is a fact; everyone does not graduate from high school. Grandma used this statement to encourage those who struggled in school. She knew sometimes telling them this would relieve the stress from what others or even themselves where causing through the constant statement, "You must Graduate with your class". Grandma believed in education but not the stress of education. Life goes on even if you did not graduate. There are other avenues to education. Life is a good teacher and the GED programs are too! Grandma also knew humankind enjoyed throwing their weight around. Some people would do well to keep their mouths close. However, no, they open them anyway. They would put themselves above others, when they discovered an individual did not graduate from High School; or they had less formal education than 'required', of course according to them. In addition, many who do not graduate with their 'high school class', look down upon themselves for the same reason. They assumed they were not of value. Grandma's requirements of us came from God. She did not judge a person according to their education. Studying comes from God and what we study should too. What we study should be life giving not life taking. As we live and are educated, we should strive towards excellent humanity, not excellence in humiliation. The system tells a person, you must get our education or you are not of value to our sociality. Then when you receive the system's education, most persons are saddled with debt, which further cast persons as less because you cannot pay and buy without struggling, even with their education. Now being educated you feel foolish. On the other hand, allowing wisdom of God to lead us into our educational choices, we gain knowledge that can never be taken away or charged as debt.

If They Make It Here
They Are Supposed
To Be Here

When I heard Grandma say this, she referred to, babies. Often time than not, people carry guilt from decisions concerning having babies or not having babies. Who has the right to have babies? Who has the right to not have babies? This was solved before the questions were asked. Grandma said if they make it here they are supposed to be here. If they do not make it here, they were chosen not to be here. Judging who makes it and why has led to many hurt feelings even death. Many deaths come in the name of God. But God who gives and takes life does not need help. God created us without help from us. So many "intelligent people" have stepped in the foot prints of the creator and tried to understand, only to misunderstand. When will human kind acknowledge, God is God all by God self.

Woman have carried the guilt of not bearing children.

Men have carried some shame of not fathering children.

When are you having children? Why haven't you had

children? Questions asked of humans by humans as if

they could make a difference in the outcome. Humans

are not the beginning and they are not the end; The

Alpha or the Omega. Beginning life is in the hand of the

life giver; as well as taking life. No man can truly give life

or take life. No man can take what he has not given. And

no man can give that which he does not have. Only

through The Creator.

If You Want To Know About Someone, Follow Them Home

People will show you who they want you to see.

Good or bad. Kind or malicious. The reality waits at

home. How they treat their love ones; the one who loves

them, will show you who they really are. Do they gripe at

them? Do they embrace them? Do they kick the family

pet? Do they have children? Is the house clean? What is the house filled with? What do you sense the moment you enter the house; is it a home? How do they answer the phone or deny calls of others in your presence. Following a person home involves looking at their heart and listening to it too! Looking at only the outer parts of a person can cause distractions of who the person really is showing you they are. In public we are on stage. Lights camera, action! In public we walk the runway! In public we dress for success! In public we mind our business! At home we are comfortable. At home we allow our hair to be down. At home we prepare to rest. At home we take off the mask literally and physically. Follow them home and see the light of who they really are. Remember home is not the TV show; that is a production.

It's Different When
It's Your Baby

Grandma said it and it did not hit me in a good way. I considered myself as the family baby sitter. I baby sat newborns and up. From the early age of 9 years I kept other people children. I treated them as if they were mine. I took great joy in knowing the parents could trust me, because I loved their child as they did in their absence. However what Grandma said on that faithful day, ruffled my feathers. She shook her head, as I offered, but Grandma I care for them as if they are mine. She quietly repeated, it's different when it's your baby. At that time my feathers ruffled because I had no intentions of birthing children. I desired to adopt as many children as I could. Years later after becoming a Mother, I could hear what Grandma said, it's different when it's your baby. Grandma was right again! Sure it is true I loved other people children as if they were mine, but they were not mine. Parenting takes 24 hour 7 days a week, not just 2 to 3, hours every now and then. This amounts to only a little while. Having my own would take something that was still locked up inside of me to be unlocked. Grandma knew my fears had over taken me and she could see the real Mother in me trying to come out. She knew having my own would be the key to my trueness. Years later Motherhood came in and hit me like a ton of rocks. The load was heavy, but I was being fitted to carry. With each pregnancy I became the person God created me to be. No more fear to drive me into thinking I am something I am not. Fear had me speaking into my future and causing a life different from God's perfect plan for me. With fear of Motherhood out of my way, my future looked brighter each day! It is different when they are mine. Thanks Grandma!

Take Them Backwards

Grandma said when she had dreams she always took them backwards to understand what they meant. You know I asked Grandma how she took her dreams backwards. Grandma simply explained, taking them backwards: replacing what she saw, heard or believed with the opposite of what she saw, heard or believed. If she saw a tree with leaves the opposite would be a tree without leaves. If she heard noises, the opposite would be no noises. If she believed what she saw, or heard the opposite would be not to believe. Instead of walking down the street she would be walking up the street; or maybe running. Then I said Grandma my dreams come true just the way I see them. Grandma gave a strange look, a chuckle and then a hug!

Write one of your dreams down, now take them

backwards.

Twelve Year Old Talk

Grandma said, once a child reaches the age of

Twelve (12), they have decided who they are. Twelve I

thought. Then I asked, Grandma why twelve. This is

what I understood. At 12 years old a child should have

been taught right from wrong. At 12, the child should

know when he or she is telling the truth verses a lie.

Those are basic skills for successful relationships. I

started what is known as "The 12 Year Old Talk". When

my nieces or nephews were around me at 12 I gave

them "The 12 Year Old Talk". This talk included:

1. The Bible Story about Jesus being found in the

    Temple at the age of 12 engaging in

    conversations with the elders. (Luke 2:41-52KIV)

2. The "Birds and The Bees"

3. Letting them know they are important to be heard even in the Temple (Church)

4. God can use anyone.

5. Even when preaching or teaching, obey your parents always during childhood like Jesus did.

Twice A Child Once An Adult

Grandma said, we live this life and if we live long enough, we will start as a child turn into an adult then, a child again. I guess I looked at Grandma the same way I suppose the people looked at Jesus when he said you must be born again. Twice a child once and adult. Okay Grandma! Grandma said yes as she further explained, we are born a baby and we need care. Diapers changed and feeding is done completely by others. We live as adults for a while. If we continue to live and become elderly adults, we will need our diapers changed and feeding done completely by others again. A Light bulb came on in my mind. I understand Grandma. Twice a

child once an adult. But, you got to keep living! Living!

Living!

About The Author

Sonya JW Lunsford is a shy person covered and dipped in the Holy Spirit. Being covered and dipped hides shy me; people really don't know about that! God's Grace and Mercy are avenues where I live. I have always enjoyed writing. Grandma said is only one of many books I am currently writing. Writing this book took me 11 months. I kept hearing my Grandma's voice. Hearing, listening and writing I would become too emotional and needed to stop writing, and just feel for a while. That is what I did. Days and weeks would go by before I could pick up the writing. Grandmas have much to say. For that I am very thankful! With every child she gave birth to, volumes were spoken. Later when the grandchildren came, series of volumes were written in Grandma. Words of wisdom and experiences of life became what is now known as, I can still hear what Grandma said "Give me my flowers while I live". Writing what Grandma said needed to happen for me because Grandma said it and I believed every word. I proved to Grandma that I believed in her by living according to what she said. I know Grandma loves me and she would never tell me anything wrong. I also felt that if by chance something was wrong with what Grandma said, God would make it right! I am not the type who has to try my way. What Grandma's said was good enough for me. But most importantly I needed to know Grandma, and knowing Grandma helped me understand and accept what Grandma said. Knowing Grandma helped me understand what God said. Knowing Grandma helped me understand myself. Knowing what Grandma said, helps me understand others. I know Grandma, is a praying woman, a woman of faith, a singer, a dancer, a clean woman, the best cook ever, a leader, a hard worker, thrifty, a giver and of course a Super Hero who loves me! Thanks to God for creating my Grandmas! They helped me handle my truth.

References

Wikipedia, the free encyclopedia 2015

Oxford Dictionary 2015

English Standard Version *(ESV)*
Old Testament
Ps. 51:10 Pg. 77
Jer. 1:9 Pg. 146

New Testament
Lk. 6:45 Pg.45

Heb. 13:16 Pg. 24

Good News Translation *(GNT)*
Heb. 4:12 Pg. 54

King James Version *(KJV)*
Old Testament
Ex. 4:21 Pg. 2

Num. 14:31 Pg. 180

Prov. 6:20 Pg. 4

New Testament
Matt. 6:9-13 Pg. 52

Matt. 18:19 Pg. 26

Matt. 18:20 Pg. 26

Lk. 2:41-52 Pg. 90

Lk. 21:34 Pg. 88

Rom.3:4 Pg. 161